INTERPRETIVE BIOGRAPHY

NORMAN K. DENZIN
University of Illinois at Urbana-Champaign

Qualitative Research Methods
Volume 17

SAGE PUBLICATIONS

ublishers
)elhi

For information address:

SAGE Publications, Inc.
2455 Teller Road
Newbury Park, California 91320
E-mail: order@sagepub.com

SAGE Publications Ltd.
6 Bonhill Street
London EC2A 4PU
United Kingdom

SAGE Publications India Pvt. Ltd.
M-32 Market
Greater Kailash I
New Delhi 110 048 India

Printed in the United States of America

Library of Congress Cataloging-in-Publication Data

Denzin, Norman K.
     Interpretive biography / Norman K. Denzin.
          p.   cm. — (Qualitative research methods ; 17)
     Bibliography: p.
     ISBN 0-8039-3358-4. — ISBN 0-8039-3359-2 (pbk.)
     1. Biography (as a literary form)   2. Autobiography.   I. Title.
     II. Series: Qualitative research methods ; v. 17.
     CT22.D45   1989
809'.93592—dc20   89-10611
                                                                     CIP

                    99   00   01   12   11   10   9   8

CONTENTS

Editors' Introduction   5

Preface   7

Acknowledgments   12

1. **Assumptions of the Method**   13

   The Subject and the Biographical Method   13
   Exemplars   14
   Situating the Method   17
   The Subject in the Text: An Aside   20
   Standards of Autobiographical Truth   23
   Recapitulation   25

2. **A Clarification of Terms**   27

   Clarifying Terms   27
   Lives, Persons, Selves, Experiences   28
   Approaches to Autobiography, Life History, and Biography   34
   Life Stories, Self Stories, and Personal Experience Stories   42
   Writing, Différence, and Presence   44
   Conclusions   47

3. **Interpretive Guidelines**   49

   Objective, Natural History Approaches   49
   The Classic Approach   50
   Problems with the Classic, Objective Approach:
      The Jack-Roller   52
   Objective Hermeneutics and Biographical Narratives   54
   Interpretive Strategies   56
   Interpretive Formats   58
   The Biographical Illusion   61
   Making Experience Come Out Right   62
   Group Storytelling   63
   Making Sense of an Individual's Life I: Sartre and Flaubert   64

	Making Sense of an Individual's Life II: Alcoholics	66
	The Progressive-Regressive Method	67
	Conclusions	68
4.	**Selves, Stories, and Experiences**	**69**
	Capturing and Studying Lived Experience	69
	The Epiphany	70
	Forms of the Epiphany	71
	The Cultural Locus of Stories	73
	Limits of the Story	74
	Process, Structure, and Stories	75
	True and False Stories?	75
	The Self-Narrative	78
	Obituaries	78
5.	**In Conclusion: Representing Lives**	**81**
	References	**85**
	About the Author	**95**

EDITOR'S INTRODUCTION

The telling of a life is an artful and selective endeavor. It involves a good deal of bold assertion and immodest neglect. Current literary and critical readings of biographies (and autobiographies) attempt to catalogue the many ways writers express singular experience and character. When these narrative devices are contrasted, distinctive forms emerge that reveal choices an author has made in the process of (re)constructing a life. As with any conventional form, the representational choices open to a writer are sometimes not seen as choices at all, such that degrees of freedom are lost, and a hardened or formula biography results. Recognizing such choice points and, perhaps, loosening up biographical genres is one of Norman Denzin's aims in this 17th Volume of the Sage Qualitative Research Methods Series. The monograph is not about using biography (i.e., as data) but about doing biography (i.e., as method). Professor Denzin is interested, then, in how lives become tales of a particular sort. This is a monograph sure to leave the reader less confident with some but better informed about all the enigmatic forms a written life can take.

—John Van Maanen
Peter K. Manning
Marc L. Miller

PREFACE

I define the biographical method as the studied use and collection of life documents, or *documents of life* (Plummer, 1983; p. 13), which describe turning-point moments in individuals' lives. These documents will include autobiographies, biographies (Dilthey, 1910/1961, pp. 85-93), diaries, letters, obituaries, life histories, life stories, personal experience stories, oral histories, and personal histories. This book is an overview and critical interpretation of the method and its uses in the human disciplines.

But it is more than this. My subject is not the use of the biographical method as a resource for sociological analysis. It is not a "how to do it" methods book. There will be no laying in of a set of procedures that a researcher might follow when attempting to do a life story or life history.[1]

My subject, instead, is how biographical texts are written and read. I deal with the forms and types of writing activity that lead to the production and analysis of biographical texts. As my definition above suggests, there are many biographical methods, or many ways of writing about a life. Each form presents different textual problems and leaves the reader with different messages and understandings.

My focus is on construction or on the doing of biography. My intentions are to come to terms with a variety of literary techniques for communicating about a life or for inscribing a body of experiences connected to the life of a given individual. I examine the inevitable shortcomings of all such techniques, contending that a life or a biography is only ever given in the words that are written about it. This, then, is an epistemological critique that has the biography as its focus.

I will be challenging conventional understandings concerning the use of this method. I am not discouraging the use of the biographical method, for, in the final analysis, it is all that we have. Instead, I want to call attention to problems that heretofore have been ignored or glossed. I want to develop a deeper appreciation of the textualizing, inscribing process, and thereby better inform the reader and writer of biographies of the problems that are always present when the method is used.

The biographical, life history, case study, case history, ethnographic method has been a part of sociology's history since the 1920s and 1930s when University of Chicago sociologists, under the influence of Park, Thomas, Znaniecki and Burgess, Blumer and Hughes were trained in the qualitative, interpretive, interactionist approach to human group life (Becker, 1966; Park, 1952, pp. 202-209; Plummer, 1983; Manning, 1987, pp. 14-18; Adler and Adler, 1987, pp. 8-20; Van Maanen, 1988, pp. 4-12; Faris, 1967; Blumer 1969, p. 1; Bulmer, 1984; Carey, 1975). Sociologists in succeeding generations turned away from the method. They gave their attention to problems of measurement, validity, reliability, responses to attitude questionnaires, survey methodologies, laboratory experiments, theory development, and conceptual indicators. Many researchers combined these interests and problems with the use of the life history-biographical method.[2] The result often produced a trivialization and distortion of the original intents of the method.

In the last decade, sociologists and scholars in other disciplines have evidenced a renewed interest in the biographical method (Adler and Adler, 1987, pp. 20-32; Douglas and Johnson, 1977; Douglas, 1985; Aladjem, 1987; McCall and Wittner, 1988). In 1978, a "Biography and Sociology" group formed within the International Sociological Association (ISA) and met in Uppsala, Sweden. In 1986, that group became a research committee within the ISA.[3] The "Biography and Society" group now publishes its own newsletter and journal, *Life Stories/Récits de vie*. The journal of the Oral History Society, *Oral History*, regularly publishes life history-biographical materials. Within sociology and anthropology, *Qualitative Sociology, The Journal of Contemporary Ethnography, Dialectical Anthropology,* and *Current Anthropology* frequently publish biographically related articles, as does *Signs* (Geiger, 1986). The autobiography has become a topic of renewed interest in literary criticism (Elbaz, 1987; Cockshut, 1984; Spengemann, 1980; Mehlman, 1974). Feminists have led the way in this discussion (Jelinek, 1980; Spacks, 1976; Springer, 1980; Clough, 1989; Stanton, 1984; Aladjem, 1987). In recent years, a number of sociological monographs using the method have appeared.[4] In short, the method has returned to the human disciplines. (Some would say it never left and that it is enjoying a "rebirth" in the late 1980s).

This project takes its direction from three sources: C. Wright Mills (1959), Jean-Paul Sartre (1971/1981), and recent developments in literary, interpretive theory (Derrida, 1972/1981). In 1959, C. Wright Mills argued (p. 6) that the sociological imagination "enables us to grasp history and biography and the relations between the two within society." He then suggested that "No social study that does not come back to the problems of biography, of history and of their intersections within a society has completed its intellectual journey" (1959, p. 6). The present work continues Mills's journey.

In the preface to volume one of *The Family Idiot: Gustave Flaubert, 1821-1857* (1971/1981, pp. ix-x) Jean-Paul Sartre asks

> what . . . can we know about man? For a man is never an individual; it would be more fitting to call him a *universal singular*. Summed up and for this reason universalized by his epoch, he in turn resumes it by reproducing himself in it as singularity. Universal by the singular universality of human history, singular by the universalizing singularity of his projects, he requires simultaneous examination from both ends. We must find an appropriate method.

Sartre's method, earlier set out in his *Search for a Method* (1963), provides a connection to Mills's injunction and will be critically examined in Chapter 3.

The last decade, as noted above, has seen a resurgence of interest in interpretive approaches to the study of culture, biography, and human group life[5]. Central to this view has been the argument that societies, cultures, and the expressions of human experience can be read as social texts, that is as structures of representation that require symbolic statement (Turner and Bruner, 1986; Bruner, 1986, p. 7; Brown, 1987, p. 119). These texts, whether oral or written, have taken on a problematic status in the interpretive project. Questions have emerged concerning how texts are authored, read, and interpreted (Derrida, 1972/1981). How authors, lives, societies, and cultures get inside interpretive texts are now hotly debated topics (Geertz, 1988). The central assumption of the biographical method, that a life can be captured and represented in a text, is now open to question. A life is a social text, a fictional, narrative production. The method of its production is primal. It is what is produced about it. Form is content. I address this issue, which has been given the term *the metaphysics of presence* (Derrida, 1972/1981) throughout this work.

This book continues themes developed in my earlier books, *On Understanding Emotion* (1984a), *The Alcoholic Self* (1987a), *The Re-*

covering *Alcoholic* (1987b), *The Research Act* (1989b, chapter 8), and *Interpretive Interactionism* (1989a), in which I attempted to articulate an interpretive approach to the use of biographical materials and the study of turning-point experiences in the lives of alcoholics, emotionally divided selves, and violent families. Here I focus solely on the method that organized these earlier works.

A basic question drives the interpretive project in the human disciplines: How do men and women live and give meaning to their lives and capture these meanings in written, narrative and oral forms? As Marx (1852/1983, p. 287) observed, men and women "make their own history, but not . . . under conditions they have chosen for themselves; rather on terms immediately existing, given and handed down to them." How are these lives, their histories, and their meanings to be studied? Who are these people who make their own history? What does history mean to them? How do sociologists, anthropologists, historians, and literary critics read, write, and make sense of these lives? These questions and others related to them organize this book.

Chapter 1 examines key assumptions of the biographical approach. A select number of texts are presented. I draw on recent literary statements on the theory of the autobiography. Chapter 2 defines key terms, including *autobiography, biography, life story, self story, case study, case history, fiction, narrative, history, oral history,* and *personal history.* Chapter 3 discusses guidelines for gathering and interpreting biographical materials. Chapter 4 takes up the concept of *epiphany,* or turning-point moments in persons' lives. It analyzes some personal experience and self stories. It examines stories within stories, and the group locus of stories. It also discusses obituaries. Chapter 5, "Conclusion," offers observations on reading and writing lives.

DEFINITIONS

AUTOBIOGRAPHY: A person's life written by oneself. Inscribing and creating a life.

AUTOBIOGRAPHY: The poor man's history (Carver, 1988c, p. 380).

BIOGRAPHY: A written account or history of the life of an individual. The art of writing such accounts.

WRITING: The work of an author creating a literary production, like a life.

INTERPRETIVE BIOGRAPHY: Creating literary, narrative, accounts and representations of lived experiences. Telling and inscribing stories.

NOTES

1. See Denzin, 1989b, chapter 8, pp. 205-209 for such a discussion.
2. See chapter 2 and the discussion of criteria.
3. See Bertaux and Kohli, 1984 for a history of the group. Also see Bertaux, 1981b, and Helling, 1988 for a history of this method's resurgence in German sociology.
4. See Plummer, 1983 for a review.
5. See Geertz, 1983; Brown, 1987; Denzin, 1989a, chapter 1; Van Maanen, 1988; and Clifford, 1988 for reviews.

ACKNOWLEDGMENTS

I would like to thank Peter K. Manning for encouraging me to do this project and for his careful reading of an earlier draft, John Van Maanen for his clarification of what I am attempting, Mitch Allen for helping me shape it, Norbert Wiley for conversations on the problem, Daniel Bertaux and the "Biography and Society" Research Committee of the International Sociological Association for being present over the last decade, Patricia Ticineto Clough and Anne Balsamo for poststructuralist, postmodern, feminist directions, Gary Krug for clarifications of the concept *epiphany,* the Unit for Criticism and Interpretive Theory at the University of Illinois for the environment which permitted these thoughts to be thought, and my wife, Katherine E. Ryan, who helped me give them whatever coherence they may have, and Richard Louisell for his assistance in proofreading.

INTERPRETIVE BIOGRAPHY

NORMAN K. DENZIN
University of Illinois at Urbana-Champaign

1. ASSUMPTIONS OF THE METHOD

The interpretive biographical method, as indicated in the preface, involves the studied use and collection of personal-life documents, stories, accounts, and narratives which describe turning-point moments in individuals' lives (Denzin, 1989a, chapter 2; 1989b, chapter 8). The subject matter of the biographical method is the life experiences of a person. When written in the first person, it is called an autobiography, life story, or life history (Allport, 1942, chapter 6). When written by another person, observing the life in question, it is called a biography. My intentions in this chapter are to offer a series of examples of autobiographical and biographical writing and then to make a number of critical points about the method and its assumptions. But, first, a brief aside.

The Subject and the Biographical Method

From its birth, modern, qualitative, interpretive sociology — which I date with Weber's meditations on *verstehen* and method (1922/1947; 1922/1949) — has been haunted by a *metaphysics of presence* (Derrida, 1972, p. 250), which asserts that real, concrete subjects live lives with meaning and these meanings have a concrete presence in the lives of these people.[1] This belief in a real subject who is present in the world has led sociologists to continue to search for a method (Sartre, 1963) that would allow them to uncover how these subjects give subjective meaning to their life experiences (Schutz, 1932/1967). This method would rely upon the subjective verbal and written expressions of meaning given by the individuals being studied, these expressions being windows into the inner life of the person. Since Dilthey (1900/ 1976), this search has led to a perennial focus in the human sciences on the autobiographical approach and its interpretive biographical variants, including hermeneutics.[2]

Derrida (1972) has contributed to the understanding that there is no clear window into the inner life of a person, for any window is always filtered through the glaze of language, signs, and the process of signification. And language, in both its written and spoken forms, is always inherently unstable, in flux, and made up of the traces of other signs and symbolic statements. Hence there can never be a clear, unambiguous statement of anything, including an intention or a meaning. My task in this book is to reconcile this concern with the metaphysics of presence, and its representations with a commitment to the position that interpretive sociologists and anthropologists study real people who have real-life experiences in the social world (Turner and Bruner, 1986; Plath, 1987).

Exemplars

Consider the following excerpts from some classic and contemporary autobiographical and biographical texts.

AUTOBIOGRAPHIES

Augustine (1960, p. 43) opens his *Confessions:*

> You are great, O Lord, and greatly to be praised: great is your power and to your wisdom there is no limit. And man who is part of your creation, wishes to praise you . . .

In her quasi-autobiographical *A Room of One's Own* (1929, p. 76), Virginia Woolf comments on the values that shaped her writing about her own life:

It is obvious that the values of women differ very often from the values which have been made by the other sex . . . it is the masculine values that prevail.

Carolyn Kay Steedman (1987, pp. 6, 7, 9) situates her life story in *Landscape for a Good Woman: A Story of Two Lives,* in her mother's life:

My mother's longing shaped my own childhood. From a Lancashire mill town and a working-class twenties childhood she came away wanting: fine clothes, glamour, money; to be what she wasn't [p. 6] . . . I grew up in the 1950s [p. 7] . . . The very devices that are intended to give expression to childhoods like mine and my mother's actually deny their expression. The problem with most childhoods lived out in households maintained by social class III (manual), IV, and V parents is that they simply are not bad enough to be worthy of attention.

John Cheever, the novelist, pays some attention to the details of his life, which might otherwise not have been worthy of attention:

I have been a storyteller since the beginning of my life, rearranging facts in order to make them more interesting and sometimes more significant. I have turned my eccentric old mother into a woman of wealth and position and made my father a captain at sea. I have improvised a background for myself—genteel, traditional—and it is generally accepted. But what are the bare facts, if I were to write them. The yellow house, the small north living room with a player piano and on a card table, a small stage where I made scenery and manipulated puppets. The old mahogany gramophone with its crank, its pitiful power of reproduction. In the dining room an overhead lamp made from the panels of a mandarin coat. Against the wall the helm of my father's sailboat—long gone, inlaid with mother of pearl (Susan Cheever, 1984, p. 12).

Stanley, the young subject of *The Jack-Roller* (Shaw, 1930/1966), perhaps the most famous sociological autobiography, and the victim of a bad childhood, starts his story with the following words:

To start out in life, everyone has his chances—some good and some very bad. Some are born with good fortunes, beautiful homes, good educated parents; while others are born in ignorance, poverty and crime. In other words, Fate begins to guide our lives even before we are born . . . My start was handicapped by a no-good, ignorant, and selfish stepmother, who thought only of herself and her own children.

Nine pages into his autobiography, *The Words* (1964/1981, pp. 18-19), Jean-Paul Sartre locates himself in the family history he has been telling:

> The death of Jean-Baptiste [his father] was the big event in my life: it sent my mother back to her chains and gave me my freedom. There is no good father, that's the rule . . . I left behind me a young man who did not have time to be my father and who could now be my son. Was it a good thing or a bad? I don't know. But I readily subscribe to the verdict of the eminent psychoanalyst: I have no Superego.

BIOGRAPHIES

Helmut R. Wagner (1983, p. 5) begins his intellectual biography of Alfred Schutz with the following lines:

> Alfred Schutz was born in Vienna on April 13, 1899. His father died before his birth, and his mother married the brother of her first husband, Otto Schutz. This man was a bank executive who secured a good middle-class existence for his family; a quiet person, he did not exert much influence on his stepson. By contrast, Schutz's mother was energetic, strong-willed, and protective. She played a decisive role in guiding her son's development . . .

Richard Ellman (1959, p. vii) describes the origins of his justly famous biography of James Joyce:

> Twelve years ago in Dublin Mrs. W. B. Yeats showed me an unpublished preface in which Yeats described his first meeting with James Joyce. My book had its origins at that time, although I did not work on it steadily until 1952.

Ellman's text (1959, p. 1) begins:

> We are still learning to be James Joyce's contemporaries, to understand our interpreter. This book enters Joyce's life to reflect his complex . . . incessant joining of event and composition.

In the next chapter, "The Family Before Joyce," Ellman (1959, p. 9) states:

> Stephen Dedalus [the hero of Joyce's *The Portrait of the Artist as a Young Man*), said the family was a net which he would fly past, but James Joyce chose rather to entangle himself and his works in it. His relations appear in his books under thin disguises.

Quentin Bell (1972, p. 1), begins his biography of his aunt, Virginia Woolf, by locating her within her family history:

> Virginia Woolf was a Miss Stephen. The Stephens emerge from obscurity in the middle of the eighteenth century. They were farmers, merchants, and receivers of contraband goods in Aberdeenshire . . . As soon as she was able to consider such things Virginia believed that she was heiress to two very different and in fact opposed traditions (p. 18).

Situating the Method

Several critical points concerning the autobiographical and biographical method may be drawn from these extended excerpts. Autobiographies and biographies are conventionalized, narrative expressions of life experiences. These conventions, which structure how lives are told and written about, involve the following problematic presuppositions, and taken-for-granted assumptions: (1) the existence of others, (2) the influence and importance of gender and class, (3) family beginnings, (4) starting points, (5) known and knowing authors and observers, (6) objective life markers, (7) real persons with real lives, (8) turning-point experiences, (9) truthful statements distinguished from fictions.

These conventions serve to define the biographical method as a distinct approach to the study of human experience. They are the methods by which the "real" appearances of "real" people are created. They are Western literary conventions and have been present since the invention of the biographical form. Some are more central than others although they all appear to be universal, while they change and take different form depending on the writer, the place of writing, and the historical moment. They shape how lives are told. In so doing, they create the subject matter of the biographical approach. They were each present in the biographical and autobiographical excerpts just presented. I will treat each in turn.

The "Other": Biographical texts are always written with an "other" in mind. This other may be God, as with Augustine; other women (Woolf and Steedman); or an intellectual or status community of abstract and specific people (Ellman, Wagner, Sartre, Cheever, Bell, Stanley). The presence of an "other" in autobiographical and biographical texts means that they are always written with at least a double perspective in mind: the author's and the other's. The eye of the other directs the eye of the writer (Elbaz, 1987, p. 14).

Gender and Class: These texts are gendered, class productions, reflecting the biases and values of patriarchy and the middle class. They are ideological statements, often representing and defending the class or gender position of the writer. But more is at issue. Until recently, women did not write autobiographies. Their lives were not deemed important enough to have biographies written about them (Steedman, 1987, p. 9). For example, William Mathew's standard bibliography of British spiritual autobiographies written during the nineteenth century lists twenty-two written by men and five by women (Peterson, 1986, pp. 120-121). Of the twenty-five individuals in Plummer's (1983, p. 15) cast of social science subjects from whom life stories were gathered, four are female subjects, an additional three are about males who were female hermaphrodites.

Family Beginnings: These productions are grounded in family, family history, the biographies and the presences and absences of mothers and fathers. It is as if every author of an autobiography or biography must start with family, finding there the zero point of origin for the life in question. Elbaz (1987, p. 70) argues that, by the eighteenth century, "this concept of zero point had extended from the realm of the individual self to that of the social whole." Davis (1986, pp. 53-54) suggests that, in sixteenth-century France, the family system played a double function of placing persons within a patriarchal structure while positioning them within a larger social field. These "family" others are seen as having major structuring effects on the life being written about, for example, Schutz's mother and stepfather or Stanley's wicked stepmother.

Textual Turning Points: By beginning the autobiographical or biographical text with family, these sources presume that lives have beginnings or starting points. But, on this, Gertrude Stein (1960, quoted by Elbaz, 1987, p. 13) reminds us:

> About six weeks Gertrude Stein said, it does not look to me as if you were ever going to write that autobiography. You know what I am going to do. I am going to write it for you. I am going to write it as simply as Defoe did the autobiography of Robinson Crusoe. And she has and this is it.

This passage appears at the end of Stein's autobiography, titled, *The Autobiography of Alice B. Toklas* (1960). Stein is telling the reader that "the beginning coincides with the end and the end with the beginning — which is the end — for autobiography (like fiction) is an act of ceaseless renewal: the story is never 'told' finally, exhaustively, completely" (Elbaz, 1987, p. 13). Stein is suggesting that the narrator or writer of an autobiography is a fiction, just as an autobiography is a fiction. That is, just as Defoe wrote a fictional autobiography of a fictional character, Robinson Crusoe, Stein has written a fictional autobiography of herself called, the autobiography of Alice B. Toklas. Stein is contending that the line between lives and fictions is impossibly and unnecessarily drawn (see discussion below).

The autobiographical and biographical genre is structured by the belief that lives have beginnings in families. Since this belief is part of the genre, virtually all biographical texts begin with family history. Stein's position challenges this conventional view concerning beginnings.

Knowing Authors: These texts presume the presence of an author or "outside" observer who can record and make sense of the life in question. If the text is autobiographical, it is assumed that the self of the writer knows his or her life, and hence is in the best position to write about it. In the biographical text, the same presumption holds, only now the interpretive work must be done by a diligent, hardworking, attentive scholar, for example, Ellman's text above.

Objective Markers: The above excerpts suggest that lives have objective and subjective markers and that these markers reflect key, critical points about the life in question. They suggest the existence of "real" persons, whose existence in a real world can be mapped, charted, and given meaning. The markers of these "real" lives may be the values that structure the text (Woolf), a working class mother's wants and desires (Steedman), the house where one grew up (Cheever), a selfish stepmother (Stanley), the death of a father (Sartre, Schutz), a writer's works (Joyce). It is assumed that these markers fit into place and give coherence to the life in question.

Sartre (1971/1981, p. ix), in his discussion of Flaubert's life, makes the following argument as he describes two pieces of information about Flaubert:

> The fragments of information we have are very different in *kind;* Flaubert was born in December 1821 . . . that is one kind of information . . . he writes, much later, to his mistress: "Art terrifies me" — that is another. The first is an objective, social fact, confirmed by official documents; the second, objective too . . . refers in its meaning to a feeling that issues from experience . . . Do we not then risk ending up with layers of heterogeneous and irreducible meanings? This book attempts to prove that irreducibility is only apparent, and that each piece of data set in its place becomes a portion of the whole, which is constantly being created, and by the same token reveals its profound homogeneity with all the other parts that make up the whole.

A life, it is assumed, is cut of whole cloth, and its many pieces, with careful scrutiny, can be fitted into proper place. But this writing of a life, Sartre suggests, like Stein, is constantly being created as it is written. Hence the meanings of the pieces change as new patterns are found.

The Subject in the Text: An Aside

Sartre's position skirts the problem of the subject's "reality" in the world of the autobiographical text. Granted Flaubert was born in December 1821, but how does Sartre get Flaubert's life into his text? This is the problem of language and writing, for, as Derrida (1981) argues, the principle knowledge of (and about) a subject only exists in the texts written about them. Sartre proclaims the existence of a "real" person, Flaubert. However, as Benveniste (1966) argues, and Derrida (1972/1981, p. 29; 1972, p. 271), develops, the linguistic concept of *person* or *subject* in language only refers to the person making an utterance, as in "I am writing this line about persons." My referentiality in the above line is only given in the pronoun *I*. My personhood is not in this line. The pronoun *I* is a shifter, and its only reference is in the discourse that surrounds it. This means, as Elbaz (1987, p. 6) argues, that "the notion of person takes meaning only within the parameters of the discursive event." My existence, or Flaubert's, is primarily, and discursively documented in the words written about or by them.

But more is involved than just the use of personal pronouns like *I*. Persons as speaking subjects (Merleau-Ponty, 1964, p. 84) are not just empty signs, created solely by the syntactical and semiological structures of language (Ricoeur, 1974, pp. 236-266).[3] Language, for the biographer and autobiographer, is not just an object or a structure "but a mediation through which and by means of which" (Ricoeur, 1974, p. 251), writers and speakers are directed toward biographically meaningful reality. What is at issue here is how the writing and speaking subject, as "the bearer of meaning" (Ricoeur, 1974, p. 246) in his or her texts, appropriates this pronoun *I,* which is an empty sign, and "posits himself [herself] in expressing himself [herself]" (Ricoeur, 1974, p. 256).

The pronoun *I* is waiting to be used by the autobiographical subject. Indeed, the genre and the larger political economy where such texts circulate dictates its use, along with its referent, *self* (see Elbaz, 1987, p. 153). But, as Benveniste (1966, p. 218) observes, "I signifies the person who is uttering the present instance of the discourse containing I." Now, while any speaker or writer can use this empty sign, when it is used by the writer of a biographical or autobiographical text, its use signifies *this* person making *this* utterance, *this* claim, or *this* statement. Behind the pronoun stands a named person — a person with a biography. When, as a writer and a speaker, this person appropriates these words and this pronoun (*I, you, he, she, me*), he or she brings the full weight of his or her personal biography to bear upon the utterance or statement in question (see Schutz and Luckmann, 1973, p. 114). The personal pronoun thus signifies this person making this utterance. It becomes a historical claim.

This is what autobiographies and biographies are all about: writers making biographical claims about their ability to make biographical and autobiographical statements about themselves and others. In this way, the personal pronouns take on semantic and not just syntactic and semiological meanings (Ricoeur, 1974, p. 256). The self, and its signifiers (*I,* etc.) thus take on a double existence in the biographical text. First, they point inward to the text itself, where they are arranged within a system of narrative biographical discourse. Second, they point outward to this life that has been led by this writer or this subject. Untangling this mediation and interaction between these two points of reference is what the above discussion has been all about.

The Real Person: When a biographer purports to be giving the "real" objective details of a "real" person's life, he or she is, in fact, only creating that subject in the text that is written. To send readers back to a "real" person is to send them back to yet another version of the fiction that is in the text. There is no "real" person behind the text, except as he or she exists in another system of discourse. But the central postulate of the biographical method (and of this book) is that there is a "real" person "out there" who has lived a life, and this life can be written about. This "real" person was born, has perhaps died, has left his or her mark on other people, and has probably deeply felt the human emotions of shame, love, hate, guilt, anger, despair, and caring for others. This feeling, thinking, living, breathing person, is the "real" subject of the biographical method.

The languages of autobiographical and biographical texts, then, cannot be taken as mere windows into the "real" world of "real" interacting subjects. These languages are only devices, tools, or *bricolages* for creating texts. The writers who use them are *bricoleurs*, or persons who use the "means at hand" to create texts which look like autobiographies or biographies (Derrida, 1972, p. 255).

Turning Points: Barely hinted at in the above excerpts, is the belief that a life is shaped by key, turning-point moments. These moments leave permanent marks. Again the author draws an example from Sartre, only now from his biography of Jean Genet (1952/1963, p. 1):

> An accident riveted him to a childhood memory, and this memory became sacred. In his early childhood, a liturgical drama was performed, a drama of which he was the officiant [one who officiates]: he knew paradise and lost it, he was a child and driven from his childhood. No doubt this "break" is not easy to localize. It shifts back and forth, at the dictates of his moods and myths, between the ages of ten and fifteen. But that is unimportant. What matters is that it exists and that he believes in it. His life is divided into two heterogeneous parts: before and after the sacred drama.

The notion that lives are turned around by significant events, what I call *epiphanies*, is deeply entrenched in Western thought. At least since Augustine, the idea of transformation has been a central part of the autobiographical and biographical form.[4] This means that biographical texts will typically be structured by the significant, turning-point moments in a subject's life. These moments may be as insignificant as Augustine's stealing pears from a pear tree and feeling guilt about the theft (Freccero, 1986, p. 23), or as profoundly moving as the scene in Genet's life described above by Sartre.

Truth: The above texts suggest that lives have objective, factually correct, "truth-like," documentary features. A person was born on such a date, died on this date, and, in between these dates, lived an important life. Cheever challenges this point, reminding the reader that facts can be altered by a storyteller in order to make them interesting and more significant. It is necessary, however, to dispense with Cheever's distinction. As suggested above, to argue for a factually correct picture of a "real" person is to ignore how persons are created in texts and other systems of discourse.

Standards of Autobiographical Truth

Various standards of truth in autobiographies have been proposed.[5] These include sincerity, subjective truth, historical truth, and fictional truth. The sincere autobiographer is assumed to be willing to tell the subjective truths about his or her life. A historically truthful statement would be one that accords with existing empirical data on an event or experience. An aesthetic truth is evidenced when "the autobiography is an aesthetic success" (Kohli, 1981, p. 70). Presumably such a work conforms to the canons of the autobiographical genre and reports the writer's life as the public wants to hear it reported. A fictional truth occurs when it is argued that the "'real' truth is to be contained in 'pure' fiction" (Kohli, 1981, p. 73).

More is at issue, however, than just different types of truth. The problem involves facts, facticities, and fiction. *Facts* refer to events that are believed to have occurred or will occur, i.e. the date today is July 27, 1988. *Facticities* describe how those facts were lived and experienced by interacting individuals (Merleau-Ponty, 1964, p. 119; Husserl, 1913/1962, pp. 184 and 410). *Fiction* is a narrative (story, account) which deals with real or imagined facts and facticities. *Truth,* in the present context, refers to statements that are in agreement with facts and facticities as they are known and commonly understood "within a community of minds" (Peirce, 1959, Volume 8, p. 18; 1958, p. 74). *Reality* consists of the "objects, qualities or events to which true ideas are" directed (Peirce, 1958, p. 74). There are, then, true and false fictions; that is, fictions that are in accord with facts and facticities as they are known or have been experienced, and fictions that distort or misrepresent these understandings. A truthful fiction (narrative) is faithful to facticities and facts. It creates verisimilitude, or what are for the reader believable experiences.

Shapiro (1968, p. 425), Pascal (1960, p. 19), and Renza (1977, p. 26) argue, and Cheever would agree that the autobiography is an imaginative organization of experience that imposes a distortion of truth.[6] Autobiographical statements are, then, viewed as a mixture of fiction and nonfiction, for each text contains certain unique truths or verisimilitudes about life and particular lived experiences.

Elbaz (1987, p. 11) quotes Renza (1977, p. 26) who claims that autobiographies are neither fictional or factual:

> We might say . . . that autobiography is neither fictive nor non-fictive. . . . We might view it . . . as a unique, self-defining mode of self-referential expression . . . that allows, then inhibits, the project of self-presentification. . . . Thus we might conceive of autobiographical writing as an endless prelude: a beginning without middle (the realm of fiction), or without end (the realm of history); a purely fragmentary, incomplete literary project, unable to be more than an arbitrary document.

Here Renza is making an unnecessary distinction between fiction and nonfiction, for all writing, as suggested above, is fictional. His other points about the autobiography warrant discussion. He assumes that there is a real self-referential self that gets expressed in the writer's text, and this self expresses itself in unique ways. What he fails to clarify is that the real, self-referential self is only present in a series of discourses about who a person is or was in the past. As Elbaz (1987, p. 12) observes, "The autobiographer always writes a novel, a fiction, about a third person," this third person being who he or she was yesterday, last year, or one hour ago. Autobiography and biography present fictions about "thought" selves, "thought" experiences, events and their meanings. Such works are tormented by the problem of getting this person into the text, of bringing them alive and making them believable. Fictions, in this sense, merely arrange and rearrange events that could have or did happen. Realist fiction, for example, presents its narrative in a way that is made to appear factual, i.e. as a linear, chronological sequence of events. Elbaz (1987, p. 1) argues, and I agree, "autobiography is fiction and fiction is autobiography: *both are narrative arrangements of reality*" (italics added).

The autobiographical and biographical forms, like all writing forms, are always *incomplete* literary productions. They are never arbitrary, as Renza argues, for no document is ever arbitrary (Elbaz, 1987, p. 12). These two forms are always a series of beginnings, which are then closed or brought to closure through the use of a set of narrative devices. These devices, called conclusions or last chapters, allow these forms to conform with the cultural myth that lives have endings,[7] and that true, complete stories about these lives have been or can be told. However, as argued above, autobiographies and biographies are only fictional statements with varying degrees of "truth" about "real" lives. True stories are stories that are believed in.

The dividing line between fact and fiction thus becomes blurred in the autobiographical and biographical text, for if an author can make up facts about his or her life, who is to know what is true and what is false? The point is, however, as Sartre notes, that if an author thinks something existed and believes in its existence, its effects are real.[8] Since all writing is fictional, made-up out of things that could have happened or did happen, it is necessary to do away with the distinction between fact and fiction (see additional discussion below).

Recapitulation

Given the above arguments, it is suggested that the following assumptions and arguments should structure the use of the biographical method in the human disciplines. The lived experiences of interacting individuals are the proper subject matter of sociology. That is, sociologists must learn how to connect and join biographically meaningful experiences to society-at-hand and to the larger culture- and meaning-making institutions of the late postmodern period (Mills, 1959; Denzin, 1989a, chap. 1; Becker, 1986, pp. 12-13). The meanings of these experiences are best given by the persons who experience them. A preoccupation with method, with the validity, reliability, generalizability, and theoretical relevance of the biographical method (Blumer, 1939 and 1979; Plummer, 1983; Kohli, 1981 and 1986; Helling, 1988) must be set aside in favor of a concern for meaning and interpretation (Denzin, 1986a, 1986b, 1986c, 1984b). Students of the biographical method must learn how to use the strategies and techniques of literary interpretation and criticism (Dolby-Stahl, 1985). They must bring their use of the method in line with recent structuralist and poststructuralist developments in critical theory (Derrida, 1967/1973; 1967/1978; 1972/1981; Frank, 1985; Jameson, 1975-1976; Denzin, 1989a, 1989b, 1989c) concerning the reading and writing of social texts. This will involve a concern with hermeneutics (Gadamer, 1975); semiotics (Barthes, 1957/1972; Manning, 1987); feminist theory (Balsamo, 1988); cultural studies and Marxism (Hall, 1980, 1987); postmodern social theory (Denzin, 1986a), and deconstructionism (Derrida, 1972/1981).

Lives and the biographical methods that construct them are literary productions. Lives are arbitrary constructions, constrained by the cultural writing practices of the time. These cultural practices lead to the inventions and influences of gendered, knowing others who can locate subjects within familied social spaces where lives have beginnings, turning points, and clearly defined endings. Such texts create "real" persons about whom truthful statements are presumably made. In fact, as argued above, these texts are narrative fictions, cut from the same kinds of cloth as the lives they tell about.

When a writer writes a biography, he or she writes him- or herself into the life of the subject written about.[9] When the reader reads a biographical text, that text is read through the life of the reader. Hence, writers and readers conspire to create the lives they write and read about. Along the way, the produced text is cluttered by the traces of the life of the "real" person being written about (Roth, 1988; Lesser, 1988).

These assumptions or positions turn on and are structured by the problem of how to locate and interpret the subject in biographical materials. This problem organizes the author's arguments throughout the remainder of this book. In the next chapter I seek to clarify a number of concepts which surround this method, its use, and its history in sociology and literature (Bertaux, 1981, pp. 7-8; Bertaux and Kohli, 1984; Helling, 1988; Plummer, 1983, chapter 2; Titon, 1980; Denzin, 1989b, chapter 8; Elbaz, 1987, chapter 1).

NOTES

1. Where one opens up this history is somewhat arbitrary. See Schutz, 1932/1967, p. 5 for a review; also Simmel, 1909/1950. Clearly, W. I. Thomas and Florian Znaniecki's multi-volumned work, *The Polish Peasant in Europe and America* (1918-1921) is part of this early concern for the subject and his or her subjective life experiences (Wiley, 1986). William James (1890) and the other American pragmatists Dewey, Peirce and Mead, also participated in this early focus on the individual and his or her presence in the world.

2. The autobiography, the root form of the biography, has been a central preoccupation of Western literature and the discourse of modernism at least since Augustine (A.D. 354-430) wrote his *Confessions*. See Elbaz, 1987, pp. vii and 18; but also see Misch, 1951, volume 1, chapter 2 for a discussion of the earlier origins of the autobiography as a literary form or genre in the ancient civilizations of the Middle East. The metaphysics of presence, coupled with the concept of a self who can write its history, has been "continuous throughout the ages" (Elbaz, 1987, p. vii; also Foucault, 1980; Derrida, 1967/1973). On

hermeneutics, see Heidegger, 1962 and Gadamer, 1975. Also see Plummer, 1983, chapter 2 for a review of the history of this method in sociology.

   3. I am indebted to Norbert Wiley for calling this Ricoeur manuscript to my attention.

   4. See Peterson, 1986, pp. 9 and 121. Peterson also notes that this concept is present in the Old Testament.

   5. See Kohli, 1981, pp. 69-72 for a review.

   6. However, see Elbaz, 1987, pp. 9-13.

   7. See Elbaz, 1987, p. 13 and the discussion of obituaries in chapter 4.

   8. See also Thomas and Thomas, 1928, pp. 571-572.

   9. Lesser (1988) notes, for example, that British and American autobiographers differ in their writing style. English writers are intimate and discreet and refer in their texts to a single author (*I*) and a single reader (*you*), while American writers anguish over who the audience is and typically speak of themselves in the third, not the first, person. She offers a cultural and class explanation of these differences, contending that the typical English autobiography reads as if it were written by a man "who has gone to Eton or Oxbridge" (Lesser, 1988, p. 26).

2. A CLARIFICATION OF TERMS

A family of terms combines to shape the biographical method.[1] In this chapter, I examine these terms and discusses the problems that surround their use. The terms are: *method, life, self, experience, epiphany, case, autobiography, ethnography, auto-ethnography, biography, ethnography story, discourse, narrative, narrator, fiction, history, personal history, oral history, case history, case study, writing presence, difference, life history, life story, self story,* and *personal experience story* (Titon, 1980). Figure 2.1 at the end of this chapter presents these concepts in summary fashion. My intentions are to do more than offer a dictionary of terms. I want to deconstruct the underlying conceptual foundations of the biographical project.

Clarifying Terms

The above terms require discussion. The word *method* shall be understood to refer to a way of knowing about the world. A way of knowing may proceed from subjective or objective grounds. Subjective knowing involves drawing on personal experience or the personal experience of others in an effort to form an understanding and interpretation of a particular phenomenon. Objective knowing assumes that one can stand outside an experience and understand it, independent of the persons experiencing the phenomenon in question. Intersubjective knowing rests on shared experiences and the knowledge gained from having participated in a common experience with another person (Denzin, 1984a, p. 133). The biographical method rests on subjective and intersubjectively gained knowledge and understandings of the life experiences of individuals, including one's own life. Such understandings rest on an interpretive process that leads one to enter into the emotional life of another. *Interpretation,* the act of interpreting and making sense out of something, creates the conditions for *understanding,* which involves being able to grasp the meanings of an interpreted experience for another individual. Understanding is an intersubjective, emotional process. Its goal is to build shareable understandings of the life experiences of another. As suggested in chapter 1, this is also called creating verisimilitude or "truth-like," intersubjectively shareable emotional feelings and cognitive understandings.

Lives, Persons, Selves, Experiences

All biographical studies presume a life that has been lived or a life that can be studied, constructed, reconstructed, and written about. In the present context, a *life* refers to two phenomena: (1) lived experiences (Merleau-Ponty, 1968, p. 256) or conscious existence, and (2) person. A person is a self-conscious being, as well as a named, cultural object or cultural creation. The consciousness of the person is simultaneously directed to "an inner world of thought and experience and to an outer world of events and experience" (Denzin, 1984a, p. 66). These two worlds, the inner and the outer, are termed the phenomenological stream of consciousness and the interactional stream of experience (Denzin, 1984a, p. 66). The phenomenological stream describes the person caught up in thoughts and the flow of inner experience. The outer, interactional stream locates the person in the world of others (Denzin, 1984a, p. 67). These two streams are opposite sides of the same process or chiasm (Merleau-Ponty, 1968), for there can be no firm dividing line between inner and outer experience. The biographical method recognizes this facticity about human existence, for its hallmark is the joining and recording of these two structures of experience in a personal document.

LIVES AND PERSONS

A person has a life or a set of life-experiences which are his or hers and no one elses. A life is lived on two levels, which this author has elsewhere (Denzin, 1986b, pp. 9-11; 1984a, pp. 80-85) termed *the surface* and *the deep.* At the surface level, the person *is* what he or she does in everyday doings, routines, and daily tasks. At the deep level, the person is a feeling, moral, sacred, inner self. This deep, inner self may only infrequently be shown to others (Denzin, 1984a, p. 159). It is assumed by users of the biographical method that this deep, inner life of the person can be captured in an autobiographical or biographical document.

A life is an unfinished project or set of projects. A person attempts to organize those projects around his or her identity or personal biography. Lives are biographical properties. They belong not just to persons, but also to larger social collectivities, including societies, corporations, and, for some, the world-system. How lives as biographical properties are owned, exchanged, discarded, managed, controlled, destroyed, assembled, wasted, talked and written about, is of central concern (Denzin, 1986c, p. 9) to students of the biographical method.

Every life is a moral, political, medical, technical, and economic production.[2] Morally, a life is given sacred meaning within the religious, legal, and political doctrines of a society (Durkheim, 1912). Politically, a life is constructed, lived, and given meaning within a matrix of micro-power relations which shape and constrain freedom and choice (Foucault, 1980, p. 201). Autobiographies and biographies are studies in morality, as well as personal and political power, fate, and social control.

When a life is written about, the story that is told may attempt to cover the full sweep of a person's experiences, or it may be partial, topical, or edited, focusing only on a particular set of experiences deemed to be of importance. Augustine's *Confessions* attempt to tell the complete story of his life. Plath's (1980) study of maturity in modern Japan draws on four fictional autobiographical and four biographical narratives of contemporary Japanese men and women confronting maturity and middle age. His focus is both edited and topical or partial.

LINEAR AND NONLINEAR LIVES

Freccero's (1986, p. 18) analysis of autobiography and narrative suggests that there may be two versions of the autobiographical narrative: the male, linear model, and the female, nonlinear, "more global accounting of a life story" (p. 18). He suggests that male life stories seem to be obsessed with order, linearity, conflict, and a struggle with separation from authority figures, often the mother or the father. Female life stories are "less obsessed with separation and struggle" (p. 18). I suspect that this is a historical matter. Those women in the late twentieth century who become more "male-like" in their work and writing careers will come to share the masculine preoccupation with struggle and separation, and this concern will become more prevalent in female life stories (Derrida, 1987; Balbus, 1986; Clough, 1989).

LIVING, EXPERIENCING, AND TELLING LIVES

Bruner (1984, p. 7) has made a useful distinction between a life as lived, a life as experienced, and a life as told. He states:

> A life lived is what actually happens. A life experienced consists of the images, feelings, sentiments, desires, thoughts, and meanings known to the person whose life it is. . . . A life as told, a life history, is a narrative, influenced by the cultural conventions of telling, by the audience, and by the social context.

Sociologists should never assume a perfect correspondence among these three forms and versions of a life; nor should they fail to make these distinctions (Bruner, 1984, p. 7). It is possible, of course, to imagine a life which is lived, experienced, and told about in a way which achieves a perfect relationship between these three terms, between the ideal and the real. As Bruner remarks (1984, p. 7), such a person would be "a letter-perfect copy of his culture, with no discrepancy between outer behavior, inner state, and how he chooses to characterize those behaviors and states in the stories told about them." There are inevitable gaps between reality, experience, and expression (Bruner, 1986, p. 7). The sociologist must be alert to these gaps, and sensitive to the ways in which persons and larger ideologies fill them in. (See the discussion of the ideological self below).

LIVES-AS-BOOKS

The product of autobiographical and biographical writing is typically a book. The book then becomes a commodified extension and representation of the life in question. The book turns the person (and the self) written about into a concrete object; an object that can be purchased, held, and read about. For example, autobiographies and biographies are two of the seven content categories used by the Book-Of-The-Month-Club when it publishes and markets its books to its membership (Radway, 1987). Its advertisement on the back cover of the July 24, 1988 *New York Times* "Book Review Section" pictures biographies and autobiographies about and by the following persons: Robert Kennedy, Jimmy Carter, Dave Winfield, Oscar Wilde, Elizabeth Taylor, Donald J. Trump, Tip O'Neill, Lee Iaccocca, Truman Capote, and Jonathan Winters. The same issue of the *New York Times* "Book Review Section" contains book reviews of new biographies and autobiographies on (and by) Rimbaud, Michael Harrington, Leonardo Da Vinci, Lady Bird Johnson, and John McGraw. In the above ways, lives-as-books circulate within the moral and political economies of a society.

On this, Elbaz (1987, pp. 152-153) has suggested:

> the autobiographical practice retains the form of a product—the self, a commodity with an exchange value. And the saleability of the self in our society makes the autobiography a productive literary form, overtaking the whole field of literature. Every politician, actor and media person writes his or her life story, not to mention literary autobiographies. One no longer has to await ripe old age to undertake this task; autobiography seems to be waiting for the man [the woman] rather than the man [the woman] for the autobiography.

SELF

Several forms of self must be distinguished: (1) the phenomenological, (2) the linguistic, (3) the material, or self-as-commodity, (4) the self-as-ideological subject, and (5) the self-as-desire.

The Phenomenological Self: This references the ideas, images, and thoughts a person has of himself or herself as a unique person. In this form, self is a "process that unifies the stream of thoughts and experiences the person has about herself around a single pole or point of reference" (Denzin, 1984a, p. 81). It is always ahead of the person in the situation. The phenomenological self is connected to the world through a circuit of selfness (Sartre, 1943/1978, pp. 155-158), or self-other interactions. The self is not in consciousness, but rather in experience and in the interpersonal relationships that bind the person to others (Sullivan, 1953).

The Linguistic Self: Self is also a linguistic, emotional, symbolic process consisting of indications and inner conversations the person directs to himself or herself (Perinbanayagam, 1985, p. 84; Blumer, 1969, p. 13). It consists of the person, as argued in chapter 1, filling in the empty personal pronouns (*I, me*) with personal, biographical, emotional meaning. This *I* of discourse always posits another person "to whom I say you and says you to me" (Perinbanayagam, 1985, p. 92).

The Material Self: Self-as-material-object consists of all the person calls his or hers at a particular moment in time. At the same time, self-as-object is commodified in the exchange relations that exist in the person's life. In its literary, sociological, biographical form, the material self is transformed, as noted above, into a book. It must be noted, however, that any written or graphic display of the self in a text (biography, autobiography) always erases or displaces the self as it is written about. The self is only in the words that are attached to it. Its presence is only established through *difference* (see discussion below).

The Ideological Self. Self-as-ideological subject is given in the broader cultural and historical meanings that surround the definition of the individual in a particular group at a particular time. Ideology (Althusser, 1971, p. 165) refers here "not [to] the system of the real relations which govern the existence of individuals, but the imaginary relation of these individuals to the real relations in which they 'live' and which govern their existence." Ideology "has the function (which defines it) of 'constituting' concrete individuals as subjects (Althusser, 1971, p. 171; de Lauretis, 1987, p. 6). The ideology which commands particular classes of individuals to write autobiographies and biographies constitutes these writers as subjects who inscribe their versions of subjectivity in the texts they produce. The autobiography (and biography) can be viewed as particular ideological state apparatuses; that is, as sites where individuals as unified, centered subjects are created (Althusser, 1971, p. 169). These writing forms and the material practices that surround them interpellate, call forth, and create particular pictures of concrete individuals as subjects.

The Self-as-Desire. Desire is that mode of self-consciousness which seeks its own fulfillment through the flesh, carnality, sensuousness, sexuality, and bodily presence of the other (Denzin, 1988, p. 75; Sartre, 1943/1956, p. 393; Hegel, 1807/1931, p. 220). Sexuality and *jouissance* (Lacan, 1977) are at the center of the self-as-desire. Desire always escapes complete fulfillment. It is experienced as a hungering, a lack, an absence. Yet the subject always returns to desire and its meanings in his or her life. Indeed, the gender socialization process leads individuals to acquire a distinct set of self-identities specific to sexual conduct, desire, and sexual activity. These personifications or images of self as male or female cluster into three categories: (1) the "good" sexual me, (2) the "bad" sexual me, and (3) the "not" sexual me (Lindesmith,

Strauss and Denzin, 1988, p. 296; Douglas and Atwell, 1988, chapter 2). It is not surprising, then, that autobiographical and biographical narratives focus, in one form or another, on sexuality, fathers, wives, husbands, and lovers. It should be clear that these several forms of the self will be present, in complex ways, in any personal document.

EXPERIENCE AND EXPRESSION

Persons as selves have experiences, *experience* referring here to the individuals meeting, confronting, passing through, and making sense of events in their lives. As Bruner (1986, p. 6) observes, experience refers to how the realities of a life present themselves to consciousness. Experiences may be problematic, routine, or ritual-like. Problematic experiences are also called *epiphanies,* or moments of revelation in a person's life. In an epiphany, individual character is revealed as a crisis or a significant event is confronted and experienced. Epiphanies often leave marks on lives, as when Jesse Jackson's name was put into nomination for the presidency of the United States by members of the 1988 Democratic Convention in Atlanta, Georgia on July 20, 1988. Students of the biographical method attempt to secure the meanings of epiphanies in the lives of the persons they study (I will discuss epiphanies in greater detail in chapter 4).

Experiences are given expression in a variety of ways, including rituals, routines, myths, novels, films, scientific articles, dramas performed, songs sung, and lives written about in autobiographies and biographies. Expressions of experiences are shaped by cultural conventions, i.e. the convention that lives have beginnings and endings. Expressions are processual activities. They turn on the performance and enactment of cultural and social texts. When performed or enacted, a text comes to constitute that which it represents; that is, the life is in the telling or the writing. Texts, as Bruner (1986, p. 7) argues, "must be performed to be experienced, and what is constitutive is the performance." This means that the expressions of lives as performed texts become socially constructed structures of meaning (Bruner, 1986, p. 7). The meaning of a life is given in the text that describes the life. This meaning is shaped by narrative convention and cultural ideology.

Viewing personal documents as conventionalized expressions of experience that differentially map reality or lives as lived suggests that we never get to the bottom of a life. We only ever get different expressions of the same (and different) experiences which are attached to the same (and different) versions of the same person.

CASES, HISTORIES, AUTOBIOGRAPHIES, BIOGRAPHIES, AND STORIES

A *case,* as indicated in Figure 2.1, describes an instance of a phenomenon. A case may be an event, a process, or a person. Often a case overlaps with a person, for example, the number of AIDS cases in a local community. *History* is an account of an event and involves determining how a particular event, process, or set of experiences occurred (Titon, 1980, p. 278). A *case history* refers to the history of an event or a process, i.e. the history of AIDS as a epidemic in the United States. A *case study* is the analysis of a single case or of multiple instances of the same process as it is embodied in the life experiences of a community, a group, or a person. My study of the liquor industry in the United States after prohibition combined a case history with a case study (Denzin, 1977, 1978).

An *autobiography,* as noted earlier, is a first-person account (which actually takes the third-person form) of a set of life experiences (Gusdorf, 1980). A *biography* is an account of a life, written by a third party. Dryden defined the word *biography* in 1683 as "the history of particular men's lives" (Titon, 1980, p. 280).[3] A biographer, then, is a historian of selves and lives. Autobiographies and biographies are structured by a set of literary, sociological, and interpretive conventions (i.e. openings, closings, linearity, objective voices, objective markers, and turning points, see chapter 1, pp. 13-27). They are formalized expressions of experience. An *auto-ethnography* is an ethnographic statement which writes the ethnographer into the text in an autobiographical manner (Crapanzano, 1980). This is an important variant in the traditional ethnographic account which positions the writer as an objective outsider in the texts that are written about the culture, group, or person in question (Geertz, 1988; Clifford and Marcus, 1986). A fully grounded biographical study would be auto-ethnographic and contain elements of the writer's own biography and personal history (Denzin, 1987a and 1987b). Such an auto-ethnography would be descriptive and interpretive (Denzin, 1989a).

Approaches to Autobiography, Life History, and Biography

It is necessary to distinguish four distinct approaches to the use and interpretation of autobiographies and biographies. The first—the one taken in this book — views autobiography as fiction and sees it as a literary and sociological form that creates particular images of subjects in particular historical moments. This author calls this the fictional-historical view.

AUTOBIOGRAPHY AS GENRE: TYPOLOGICAL VIEW

The second approach sees autobiography as a particular genre, style, or form, canonizes that form, and seeks to locate its origins in a pivotal text, like Augustine's *Confessions, The Polish Peasant,* or *The Jack-Roller.* This view dates the beginning of the genre with an original text and compares all subsequent representations of it to the canonizing text.[4] Thus, sociologists compare contemporary life histories and sociological autobiographies to their earliest version.

Listen to Plummer (1983, p. 16) discussing the life history in sociology:

> In sociology the method was established with the 300 page story of a Polish emigre to Chicago, Wladek Wisniewski. It was one volume of . . . *The Polish Peasant in Europe and America.* . . . Broadly, Wladek describes the early phases of his life . . . his early schooling, his entry to the baker's trade, his migration to Germany to seek work, and his ultimate arrival in Chicago and his plight there. . . . A very good modern illustration of this sociological life history research is the story of Jane Fry, a transsexual born a 'biological male' but believing she was a woman. It was gathered by Robert Bogdan largely through 100 hours of informal . . . discussions . . . transcribed into 750 pages and then edited by Bogdan. . . . The final book, Jane's story, has been organized into seventeen chapters and 200 pages.

Here Plummer traces a modern version of the life history back to its sociological original. He shows what was in the original — details about Wladek's life from childhood to adulthood. He documents the location of this new text in the genre through the 100 hours of discussion Bogdan and Jane had together (Bogdan, 1974). He anchors the text in the 750 pages of transcribed discussions and then contends that Jane's story is now told in seventeen chapters and 200 pages. It's not clear how Jane's story differs from Bogdan's story, just as it is not clear how Jane's life was told.

Elbaz (1987, pp. 1-3) terms this the typological approach. It could also be called the generic view. It suffers from a number of flaws. First, it fails to consider the point that a genre is itself a social construction; there is nothing sacred or fixed about the original version of a text or type of texts in a sequence of texts. After all, the original text in a genre is itself a version of another, earlier text. This interpretation, however, argues that there is a true beginning of the genre. All that happens after this beginning simply repeats the original version. Second, the typological approach freezes any instance of an autobiography within the genre. It isolates a number of conditions that define the form and then asks if this instance reproduces and conforms to the criteria of the form.

Sociologists, for example, are fond of delineating criteria for life histories and then judging documents in terms of these criteria (Denzin, 1989b, p. 205). For example, Dollard, writing in 1935, listed seven criteria for the life history. These were: (1) The subject is viewed as a specimen in a cultural series. (2) Organic motivation is established. (3) The role of family in transmitting culture must be established. (4) Organic materials must be related to social behavior. (5) Experience from childhood through adulthood must be stressed. (6) The social situation must be studied. (7) The life history material must be organized and conceptualized (Plummer, 1983, p. 49; Allport, 1942, p. 37; Dollard, 1935, p. 34). Dollard then evaluated six cases against these criteria. Plummer (1983, p. 50) suggests that "The discussion by Dollard may be due for resuscitation." He then proceeds (p. 103) to offer how own criteria for judging bias in the information given by an informant and then suggests (pp. 119-134) how these materials may be theorized. He thus stays within the genre, as he attempts to canonize the criteria by which such work is to be judged.

The third problem with the typological, generic approach is the frequent assumption that the life history document maps reality and, thus, is to be distinguished from fiction. Plummer's concerns with bias, validity, and reliability (1983, pp. 101-104) reflect this preoccupation with truth and the canons of science. Fourth, the typological, genre approach reproduces the concern for linearity in life histories. This is evident in Dollard's criteria concerning childhood and adulthood and the links between these two life-phases. Fifth, by making the form static, the typological position ignores the fact that each instance of the genre is only an instance which establishes the genre itself. That is, every instance changes the genre while it establishes its so-called existence in the sociological literature. Sixth, the genre approach fails to consider how subjects and authors are created by specific ideologies in specific historical moments. It assumes that authors of autobiographies and life histories have been the same since time immemorial.

AUTOBIOGRAPHY AS GENRE: COMMONSENSE VIEW

Unlike the typological position, which sees the autobiography being born in an original, fixed text, the third approach sees the "genre as a transcendental structure moving with historical fluctuations" (Elbaz, 1987, p. 3). In this view, autobiographical texts are governed by a series of constitutive rules concerning the obligations of the writer to create a coherent text about a specific individual. This text is assumed to be truthful, factually accurate, and verifiable by a reading audience (Bruss, 1976, pp. 5-7). Like the typological view, this perspective, which Elbaz calls dynamic, and this author terms commonsense, uncritically accepts the genre notion of autobiography. "It does not question the genre itself" (Elbaz, 1987, p. 9). Nor does it examine autobiographies as ideological statements. The emphasis on constitutive rules assumes that a real person's life can be accurately told about. The problems with this assertion were discussed in chapter 1. The dynamic, commonsense approach remains trapped within a positivist, scientistic conception of lives and texts. It fails to see autobiography as narrative fiction.

AGNES AND COMMONSENSE VIEWS OF LIVES IN AUTOBIOGRAPHIES AND LIFE HISTORIES

Garfinkel's (1967, pp. 111 and 288) reading of the case history of Agnes, an "intersexed" person, calls attention to the problems of the constitutive-rule, commonsense approach to autobiography. This life history of Agnes (Garfinkel, 1967, pp. 116-185) was based on thirty-five hours of conversation with the subject over a several month period (November 1958-March 1959). The life history document detailed how the subject, raised as a boy, managed a sex change from male to female. In interviews, she denied ever having taken estrogens which would have facilitated her sex change, which was accomplished in 1959 through an operation when she was nineteen years old. Nearly eight years later, in October of 1966, Agnes returned to her physician and "disclosed to him that she was not a biologically defective male" (Garfinkel, 1967, p. 285). She also revealed that she had "never had a biological defect that had feminized her but that she had been taking estrogens since age twelve" (Garfinkel, 1967, p. 287). She had duped Garfinkel and her physicians.

On this Garfinkel (1967, p. 288) remarks:

> If the reader will re-read the article in light of these disclosures, he will find that the reading provides an exhibit of . . . the recognizedly rational accountability of practical actions [as] a member's practical accomplishments, and . . . that the success of that practical accomplishment consists in the work whereby a setting . . . masks from member's relevant notice . . . a setting's features, which include . . . accounts as 'determinant and independent objects.'

That is, observers are led to believe that people are who they present themselves as being; but Agnes was not who she said she was. Nor did she accurately report her experiences. Garfinkel and his associates saw the woman they wanted to see. Who was (is) the real "Agnes?" In writing a biography and life history that conformed to the criteria of the dynamic, constitutive approach, Garfinkel produced a document that told the story Agnes wanted told. He, in fact, wrote a fiction that, until Agnes' disclosure, had the appearance of truth.

SOCIOLOGICAL AUTOBIOGRAPHIES

The fourth interpretive approach to the autobiography and the life history is sociological. This approach takes two forms: sociologists writing about their own lives, and sociologists writing about the lives of other people. The first form (Horowitz, 1969) involves sociologists-as-biographers turning the sociological imagination toward their own lives. Horowitz's collection of sociological self-images provides an instance of this version of the genre. It involved a number of prominent sociologists (including Wendell Bell, Joseph Berger, Amitai Etizioni, George Caspar Homans, Raymond Mack, Charles Moskos, and William Foote Whyte) reflecting on five questions: (1) the uniquely defining characteristics of your way of doing sociology; (2) your current relationship to sociological theory; (3) the sociologists whom you respect the most; (4) which of your writings you like the best; (5) what impact your work has had on reshaping the field (Horowitz, 1969, p. 10).

Here is an example from George Caspar Homans's statement, "A Life of Synthesis" (1969, p. 13):

> My great interest and pleasure in life is bringing order out of chaos . . . I see this trait in the long weekends I have spent on my fifty-four acres of land at Medfield, Massachusetts . . . For years I have tried to organize this

abandoned farm, now grown up to blueberry pasture and second-growth trees ... into what I call a walking woods. ... My compulsion is ... to bring order ... to some chaotic whole. ... This effort has been characteristic of my work in sociology from the beginning.

Homans goes on to state that he sees this characteristic in his first book, *An Introduction to Pareto.* He then states that Pareto is one of the sociologists who influenced him the most, that his favorite book of the books he has written is *English Villagers,* that he has endeavored to get sociologists to understand what a theory is, and that some progress has been made in this direction, "but I dare say it was not my fault ... one cannot both accomplish something and get the credit for it" (Homans, 1969, p. 31).

In these words, Homan's locates himself in his land, in his books, and in his efforts to teach sociologists how to write and understand theory. He is outside himself, in other things. Yet he sees these other things as instances of who he is and of what he has done.

Here is another sociologist writing about his career:

It is not irrelevant to point out that I was born in an Illinois prairie farmhouse on land homesteaded by my great grandfather and in the same house in which my mother was brought into this world some twenty-four years earlier (Short, 1969, p. 117).

Short returns to family beginnings and, like Homans, to the land. It is as if each writer must first find a firm anchor for his life, before he can begin writing about it. But more is going on in these passages. These sociologists-as-self-biographers assume that they are producing a document that is part of the autobiographical genre, and they are conforming to the canons of that genre as they answer Horowitz's questions. They assume that the "itness" or essence of their lives can be captured in their works. They take for granted the fact that they are real people who have had a real impact on the works of others. They go to great length to factually date their beginnings and to assure their readers that they are telling the truth about their lives (Homans, 1962, pp. 1-49). Short (1969, p. 131) states in this regard:

I confess to a good deal of ambivalence concerning this exercise in baring one's sociological (and inevitably personal) soul. It is almost too painful.

These sociologists-as-autobiographers have no sense of autobiography as fiction.

Now consider sociologists writing biographies of others. Here is Don Martindale (1981, pp. 310-311) writing about George Caspar Homans. The text is accompanied by a photograph of Homans's face.

> George Caspar Homans (1910-) was born in Boston. He earned the A.B. at Harvard College in 1932 in English literature, but found himself unemployed when a prospective job in journalism with William Allen White of the Emporia, Kansas *Gazette* failed because of the depression. He entered the famous seminar (fall 1932) of Lawrence Joseph Henderson at Harvard on Vilfredo Pareto, and started on the course that would both bring him into sociology and thrust him to the center of an emerging school of sociological theory that came to be known as structure-function-alism. Homans reports that as a self-satisfied Bostonian from a wealthy family, he was drawn to Pareto's anti-Marxism.

This is standard sociological biography. It follows the format of the genre-driven, commonsense, constitutive approach. It locates beginnings and turning points (Homans not getting the journalism job in 1932, entering Henderson's seminar). It deals with dates. It anchors the subject in a larger, socio-historical context, including the depression, Boston upper-class life, and the intellectual climate at Harvard in the early 1930s.

Sociological biography and autobiography as intellectual history merge personal lives with the world of ideas (Lemert, 1986). Subjects are located in ideas, i.e. Homans in his anti-Marxism. These ideas are assumed to have a presence in the real world. They are located in persons and in the books and classes they teach. A sociologist's intellectual life somehow appears in and becomes part of this field of discourse. In order to write about their lives, sociologists must write about these ideas and their material expressions in the real world. It is as if each sociologist is a master of the ideas that have shaped his or her life. Thus, a peculiar sociological determinism drives the sociological life history. As the master of sociological discourse, the sociologist rises above his or her own sociological life conditions to become the sociologist of his or her own (or others') lives (Coser, 1986; Merton and Riley, 1980). The sociologist-as-biographer assumes an unwarranted objectivity about his or her life and the lives of others. No writer can ever step outside history and objectively view his or her own or any other person's life (Merleau-Ponty, 1964, p. 109). By writing about lives the way they do, sociologists reify the sociological concept of the individual. In so doing, they perpetuate the illusion that sociological facts take precedence over, and are therefore unlike, fictional, literary narratives. They also perpetuate the belief that there is a unique sociological method for writing about lives and life histories.

STORIES

Ethnographies, biographies, and autobiographies rest on *stories* which are fictional, narrative accounts of how something happened. Stories are fictions. A *fiction* is something made up or fashioned out of real and imagined events. History, in this sense, is fiction. A *story* has a beginning, a middle, and an end. Stories take the form of texts. They can be transcribed, written down, and studied. They are *narratives* with a plot and a story line that exists independent of the life of the storyteller or *narrator.* Every narrative contains a reason or set of justifications for its telling (Culler, 1981, p. 187). Narrators report stories as narratives. A story is told in and through *discourse,* or talk, just as there can be discourse about the text of a story. A text can be part of a larger body of discourse. For example, Peterson's (1986) discourse on the Victorian autobiography is about specific Victorian autobiographies including Carlyle's and Ruskin's. Her book is a discourse on these books. At the same time, Carlyle's autobiography is situated within a specific textual tradition. Hence, there is always discourse about discourse. Texts are always part of larger, intertextual traditions and genres (Kristeva, 1974, pp. 59-60).

A *life history* or *personal history* is a "written account of a person's life based on spoken conversations and interviews" (Titon, 1980, p. 283). In its expanded form, the life history may pertain to the collective life of a group, organization, or community. Heyl's (1979) *The Madam as Entrepreneur: Career Management in House Prostitution* is both a personal history of Ann, the house madam, and a life history of her house of prostitution and houses of prostitution in the midwest. In this sense, her life history merges a personal history with a case history and a case study. An *oral history* focuses "chiefly on events, processes, causes, and effects rather than on individuals whose recollections furnish oral history with its raw data" (Titon, 1980, p. 291). Since oral histories are typically obtained through spoken conversations and interviews, they often furnish the materials for life histories and case histories. The journal of the Oral History Society, *Oral History*, and the journal *Life Stories/Récits de vie*, published by the Biography and Society Research Committee of the International Sociological Association, regularly publish oral history, life history, and life story studies. Oral histories should not be confused, however, with personal histories, for the latter attempt to reconstruct lives based on interviews and conversations (Denzin, 1989a, p. 186). Life histories and personal histories may be topical, focusing on only one portion of a life, or complete, attempting to tell the full details of a life as it is recollected (Neal, 1988).

Life Stories, Self Stories, and Personal Experience Stories

Life stories examine a life, or a segment of a life (Bertaux, 1981a, pp. 7-9), as reported by the individual in question. As Titon (1980, p. 276) suggests, it is "a person's story of his or her life, or of what he or she thinks is a significant part of that life. It is therefore a personal narrative, a story of personal experience." A life story may be written or published as an autobiography. Its narrative, storytelling form, gives it the flavor of fiction, or of fictional accounts of what happened in a person's life.

THE LIFE STORY AUTHOR

The life story turns the subject into an author, an author or authoress being one who brings a story into existence. The subject-as-author is given an authority over the life that is written about. After all, it is his or her life. This means the author has an authority in the text that is given by the very conventions that structure the writing or telling of the story in the first place. But where in the text of the story is the author? Clearly he or she is everywhere and nowhere. For an author is always present in personal name and signified in the words that he or she uses. But the author is not in those words; they are only signs of the author, the self and the life in question. They are inscriptions on and of the self or life that is being told about. The author is in the text only through the words and the conventions he or she uses. The languages of biography structure how biographies are written. There is no fixed, ever-present author, "no subject who is agent, author" (Derrida, 1972/1981, p. 28; See the discussion of différence below).

SELF STORIES

Self stories are told by a person "in the context of a specific set of experiences" (Denzin, 1989a, p. 186). Here is an example. The speaker is a recovering alcoholic commenting on his "using days."

> I would get up, depressed as hell. Roll a joint and grab a beer, lay back. Get in touch with the universe. I'd fly off, out of my apartment, into space, in tune with the world. No worries, no fears. I knew everything. I had all the answers. Turn the music on high, the Stones, mellow out. No depression. I called it getting in touch with the universe. Today that all sucks (Denzin, 1987a, p. 198).

A self story positions the self of the teller centrally in the narrative that is given. It is literally a story of and about the self in relation to an experience — in the above case, getting high, listening to the Stones, and being mellow. The self story is made up as it is told. It does not exist as a story independent of its telling; although, after it has been told, it can take on the status of a story that can be retold. Its narrative form typically follows the linear format, i.e. beginning, middle, end. These tellings build on the assumption that each person is a storyteller of self experiences. These oral histories of self are often mandated by social groups. Alcoholics in Alcoholics Anonymous are expected to be able to tell self stories (Denzin, 1987b, pp. 167-168). Self stories are personal narratives and may take the form of personal experience narratives.

PERSONAL EXPERIENCE NARRATIVES

Personal experience narratives are "stories people tell about their personal experience" (Stahl, 1977, p. 7; Dolby-Stahl, 1985, p. 48; Denzin, 1989b, p. 186). They often draw upon the public, oral storytelling tradition of a group. Here is an example:

> When we lived in Michigan . . . we had this great big barn. It had three hay mows . . . and way up at the top were two big cupolas — and of course the birds perched up there. But to get up there you'd have to climb into the hay mow, then they had this . . . real rickety old ladder . . . and the last step . . . was wider than the rest. . . . So we were playing hide-and-seek . . . and I decided that . . . I was going to hide up in that cupola . . . I must have been nine, ten years old . . . so I got up there . . . and they couldn't find me . . . so they started playing something else. So I began to yell . . . and . . . went to get down . . . and here this great big yard-wide step . . .

and I just couldn't step over that . . . I was too scared. . . . Lester finally decided to climb up there . . . and then I crawled over his back (Stahl, 1977, p. 23).

This story was told to the folklorist Sandra K. D. Stahl, her sister, and three of her sister's children on October 14, 1973. It is based on personal experience. It has the narrative structure of a story, i.e. a beginning, a middle, and an end. It describes a set of events that exist independent of the telling; her brother Lester could have told a different version of the story. The experiences that are described draw their meaning from the common understandings that exist in a group, although they do express the "private" folklore or meanings of the teller. When told, they create an emotional bond between listener and teller. "They express a part of the 'inner life' of the storyteller" (Dolby-Stahl, 1985, p. 47).

Personal experience narratives differ from self stories in several ways. These narratives do not necessarily position the self of the teller in the center of the story, as self stories do" (Denzin, 1989b, p. 187), although they may. Their focus is on shareable experience. Personal experience narratives are more likely to be based on anecdotal, everyday, commonplace experiences, while self stories involve pivotal, often critical life experiences. Self stories need not be coherent, linear, accounts. They need not entertain or recreate cherished values and memories of a group, while personal experience narratives do (Stahl, 1977, p. 19). Self stories, as noted above, are often mandated by a group; personal experience narratives are not. Self stories are often told to groups, while personal experience narratives may be told only to another individual. These two biographical forms are alike, however, in that they both rest on personal experiences (Denzin, 1989b, p. 187).

Writing, Différence, and Presence

The commonsense view understands writing to be a form of communication where, through the use of language, words, phrases, and often sentences, a writer conveys meanings and understandings. In this view, a word or a printed line functions to clearly convey meaning that is different from other words and other lines. A written text, then, is a bounded unit of meanings. Its meanings are clearly discernible. The text can be easily distinguished from other texts.

Derrida (1972/1981, p. 26) has challenged this position. He suggests that language is only *différence*. A word, he contends, can never function

> without referring to another element which itself is not simply present. This interweaving results in each 'element' . . . being constituted on the basis of the trace within it of the other elements of the . . . system. This interweaving . . . is the *text* produced only in the transformation of another text. . . . Nothing . . . is anywhere ever simply present or absent. There are only, everywhere, differences and traces of traces" (italics in original).

If words are only made up of différence—if signs have no stable meanings, but only exist in transformations and traces—then texts have no center or essential structure. However, stories and texts are written "as if" they do have centers. Thus, writers and readers presume and "read into" texts real authors, real intentions, and real meanings. According to Derrida, these efforts are driven by the fallacies of presence that underwrite Western metaphysics, literature, and science. That is, logocentric, subject-centered texts are written because authors and readers believe that real subjects can be found in the real world and then relocated in texts.

The logocentric bias carries a number of other assumptions. First, texts are often written in terms of implicit (and explicit) hierarchies and oppositions, i.e. self and other, the deviant and society, reason and emotion. These hierarchies and oppositions structure the text and give it a sense of order that it would not have if these oppositions were not in place.

Second, texts are written and read as if they have essential cores of meaning. Autobiographies center a person at the heart of the life story that is told. But this center, the person, is always someplace else, in a set of personal experiences, for example, in the experiences created by a wicked stepmother, in an absent father. Thus, the center is often to be found in the oppositions the text creates between the subject and his or her family.

Third, conventional readings of biographical documents seek to give a material presence to subjects, finding persons in their works, their letters, their diaries, or their relations with others. The subject is reified in material things. Fourth, in order to locate an individual's works and their meanings in a social context, authors are led to invent a version of society in which the subject and his or her works exist and are given meaning. This can be seen in a number of the excerpts discussed in chapter 1. Steedman locates her mother in working-class, British society. She locates herself in the same society in the 1950s. Wagner locates Schutz in turn-of-the-century Vienna. Quentin Bell places Virginia Woolf in the middle class, agrarian, merchant society of eighteenth century England. However, in no case does the biographer do any more than evoke this picture of society. Biographers need society in order to locate their subject, but society, as it is lived, experienced, and talked about — "real, immortal ordinary society" (Garfinkel, 1988, p. 103) — is not discussed. Society is brought in as a set of oppositions, differences, and absent presences. This gives the subject of the biography a fixed presence that could otherwise not be given.

Fifth, biographical writers must invent an intentional author and a subject whose material presence can be documented, but this invention of the subject only occurs through the invention and invocation of absent others, absent and present social structures, and so on. In short, the subject's real presence is only in the text. Sixth, once the subject is created, the biographer must ascribe to him or her a set of intentions which are displayed in his or her material works, but these intentions can only be read off of the material works. Hence, the intentional subject is both in his or her works and not in his or her works. This means that the subject is already de-centered in other places, even as the biographer seeks to anchor him or her in material texts.

Seventh, to the degree that biographers de-center their subjects, the other sites where subjects appear must be analyzed. When such analyses are performed, it will be found that the subject exists only in the traces and differences that connect these sites and their expressions to one another.

Derrida's deconstruction project challenges the above assumptions. It attempts to show how these subject-centered assumptions undermine texts and give them a "presence" that is unwarranted. His work suggests that essentialist, materialist, consensual readings of autobiographies and biographies be abandoned. In their place must emerge deconstructionist readings which are always playful, open-ended, and inconclusive. No reading or writing of a life is ever complete or final. *We must prevent words like autobiography, biography, and biographical method from assuming a force which gives a presence to a centered-life that it cannot have.* That is, these words have the potential of creating unwarranted meanings in the mind of the reader (and the writer) concerning a project which can never fulfill the aims contained in the words *autobiography* and *biography*. After all, there can only be multiple versions of a biography or autobiography.

But readers create texts, for meaning is not just in a text or in a word; it arises out of the interactions between texts, writers, and readers. This is why the framing of a text with words like *biography* and *autobiography* is so critical. These framing words shape reader interactions with texts.

It will be necessary, in the chapters that follow, to show how this conventional view of writing and subjects structures, while it undermines from within, the very essence and purpose of the biographical project.

Conclusions

I have now discussed the major terms that surround and define the biographical method. It should be clear that every term carries traces of other terms. Thus, oral histories, personal histories, and case histories, like autobiographies and biographies, and self stories and personal experience narratives, define one another only in terms of difference. The meanings of each spill over into the meanings of the other. The attempt to give a fixed meaning to each term is doomed to failure. It represents a logocentric, scientific bias that must be overcome and displaced. The very word *biographical,* implying as it does the ability to write or inscribe words on a life, eludes fixed meaning, for lives, like words, exist only in traces, spaces, and difference.

The following figure summarizes the concepts and terms that have historically defined the biographical method.

Term/Method	Key Features	Forms/Variations
1. Method	A way of knowing	Subjective/objective
2. Life	Period of existence; lived experiences	Partial/complete/edited/ public/private
3. Self	Ideas, images, and thoughts of self	Self-stories, auto-biographies
4. Experience	Confronting and passing through events	Problematic, routine, ritual
5. Epiphany	Moment of revelation in a life	Major, minor, relived, illuminative

Figure 2.1 Terms/Forms and Varieties of the Biographical Method

Term/Method	Key Features	Forms/Variations
6. Autobiography	Personal history of one's life	Complete, edited, topical
7. Ethnography	Written account of a culture or group	Realist, interpretive, descriptive
8. Auto-ethnography	Account of one's life as an ethnographer	Complete, edited, partial
9. Biography	History of a life	Autobiography
10. Story	A fiction, narrative	First or third person
11. Fiction	An account, something made up, fashioned	Story (life, self)
12. History	Account of how something happened	Personal, oral, case
13. Discourse	Telling a story, talk about a text, a text	First or third person
14. Narrator	Teller of a story	First or third person
15. Narrative	A story, having a plot and existence separate from life of teller	Fiction, epic, science, folklore, myth
16. Writing	Inscribing, creating a written text	Logocentric, de-constructive
17. Différence	Every word carries traces of another word	Writing, speech
18. Personal History	Reconstruction of life based on interviews and conversations	Life history, life story
20. Oral History	Personal recollections of events, their causes and effects.	Work, ethnic, religious, personal, musical, etc.
21. Case History	History of an event or social process, not of a person	Single, multiple, medical, legal
22. Life History	Account of a life based on interviews and conversations	Personal, edited, topical, complete
23. Life Story	A person's story of his or her life, or a part thereof	Edited, complete, topical, fictional
24. Self Story	Story of self in relation to an event	Personal experience, fictional, true
25. Personal Experience Story	Story about personal experience	Single, multiple episode, private, or communal folklore
26. Case Study	Analysis and record of single case	Single, multiple

Figure 2.1 (Continued)

NOTES

1. This chapter draws from and extends Denzin (1989b, chapter 8 and Figure 8.1, p. 188).
2. See de Lauretis, 1987, pp. 1-3, with specific reference to the gendered, technological reproduction of women and their lives in Western culture.
3. Note the sexist bias in this definition, as if women in the 1600s in England did not have lives worthy of histories.
4. For recent rereadings of sociology's canonical text, *The Polish Peasant*, see Wiley, 1986; Zaretsky, 1984; Corradi, 1987; and the papers in Dulczewski, 1986.

3. INTERPRETIVE GUIDELINES

Biographies and autobiographies must be organized and interpreted. In this chapter, I review several guidelines that have been proposed for the ordering and interpreting of life history, life story, autobiographical, and biographical materials.[1] These guidelines may be placed into one of two categories: objective formats or interpretive frameworks which work from the subject's point of view. Within the objective format category, two distinct approaches may be distinguished: the classic, objective, natural history approach associated with the Chicago School and the objective hermeneutics position of the "new" school of German life history researchers (Helling, 1988).

Traditionally, users of the objective approaches have judged their efforts in terms of the norms of validity, reliability, truth, falsity, bias, data, hypotheses, theory, case representativeness, and generalizability (Helling, 1988, pp. 230-232; Kohli, 1981, pp. 69-72; Denzin, 1989b, p. 195). Interpretive approaches reject these norms of evaluation and regard biographical materials from within a literary, fictional framework (Dolby-Stahl, 1985; Denzin, 1984a, 1985, 1986a, and 1986b).

Objective, Natural History Approaches

The classic statements of the objective, natural history approach were given by Thomas and Znaniecki (1918, Volume 1, pp. 20-28; 1919, Volume 3, pp. 5-10), Blumer (1939), Allport (1942), Gottschalk, Kluckhohn, and Angell (1945), Burgess (1930/1966), Shaw (1930/1966), Dollard (1935), Young (1952), and Lemert (1951).

The Classic Approach

Elsewhere (Denzin, 1970, pp. 236-254; 1978, pp. 247-248; 1989b, pp. 177-184) I summarized these classic formulations and presented a version of the natural history approach. I will briefly review and criticize that discussion. I argued (Denzin, 1989b, p. 184) that a life history report should be organized in terms of the following steps: (1) Select a series of research hypotheses and problems to be answered. Formulate tentative operationalizations of key concepts, then select a subject and a research site. (2) Record the objective events and experiences in the subject's life that pertain to the research problem. (3) Triangulate these events by source and point of view so that contradictions, irregularities, and discontinuities can be established. (4) Obtain the subject's interpretations of these events as they occurred in their chronological or natural order. Analyze these reports in terms of (5) the concepts of internal validity, internal criticism, external validity, and external criticism. Next (6) resolve the validity of the above sources and establish the priority of the sources for testing hypotheses. Begin (7) testing hypotheses, while searching for negative evidence and (8) organizing the initial draft of the entire life history, submitting this to the subject for reactions. Finally (9), rework the report in its natural sequence in light of these reactions. Present the hypotheses that have been supported. Conclude with a statement concerning theory.

These nine steps contain all the essential features of the classic natural history approach. They build on the position that lives have natural histories that unfold over time and that these lives are marked by objective events and experiences. A life is pictured as an orderly production. The steps are driven by a hypothesis-testing, theory-development concern. They assume that hypotheses can be operationalized. They are preoccupied with objective events and subjective definitions of these events. They presume that accurate, truthful, valid, consistent interpretations of events can be given.

Clifford R. Shaw (1930/1966, p. 21), the collector and editor of *The Jack-Roller,* describes how this life history record is to be obtained:

> The story should be as spontaneous as possible and always follow the natural sequence of events in the life of the delinquent. . . . we hoped to be able to describe . . . the natural process involved in the development of his delinquent-behavior. . . . The technique . . . is that of the personal

interview. . . . In most . . . cases a stenographic record of the interview is made . . . thus . . . its objectivity is preserved . . .

Earlier in *The Jack-Roller*, Shaw (1930/1966, p. 2) discusses how these materials are to be judged. He suggests that family history, medical, psychiatric, and psychological findings on the subject be collected as should, in the case of delinquents, the official record of arrest, offenses and commitments, play-group relationships, and

> any other *verifiable* material which may throw light upon the personality and actual experiences of the delinquent. . . . In the light of such supplementary material, it is possible to evaluate and interpret more accurately the personal document. It is probable that in the absence of such additional case material any interpretation of the life-history is somewhat questionable (Shaw, 1930/1966, p. 2, italics added).

In short, lives are verifiable concerns, and lacking verification of a subject's account, interpretations should be withheld. Furthermore, all corners and edges of a life should be nailed down. Objective documents mapping the life can then be produced. Shaw invokes others who can confirm Stanley's presence in the world. An implicit opposition between Stanley, his family history, and the reports of physicians, psychiatrists, and the courts is suggested.

Yet it is assumed that the "real" Stanley's life-history lies somewhere in the convergences that connect these documents. Shaw has centered and then de-centered Stanley, hoping to find the "real" Stanley in the verifiable materials that "throw light upon" his personality and his actual experiences. But what is the truth about Stanley? Where is he? Is he in these other materials? Is he to be found in his personality? Or is he, as Burgess (1930/1966, p. 189) suggests, to be found in "his reactions to the events of his experience." Burgess comments:

> Granted that Stanley told the truth about himself, as he sees it, the reader will have still a further question, What were the facts as they are about Stanley's stepmother . . . the House of Correction. . . . The absolute truth about these or other points cannot be secured by the life-history method and probably cannot be obtained by any other known method. But in human affairs it is not the absolute truth . . . that concerns us, but the way in which persons react to that event (Burgess, 1930/1966, p. 189).

So Stanley is to be found in his reactions to events: broken homes, poverty, bad housing, bad companions, a criminal career, the discrimination of his stepmother, the patterns of stealing prevalent in his neighborhood, "the dynamic relationship between [his] personality and his varied and stimulating experiences" (Burgess, 1930/1966, p. 189).

I am not quarreling with the position that the definitions of situations are what count. What is at issue is how these situations get into the text. However, if only definitions matter, then why the preoccupation with verifiable statements? The answer is clear. In order to create Stanley, Shaw and Burgess must anchor him in a social world filled with others. Stanley exists in the oppositions that connect him to this "mythical" world of "otherness." While Burgess (and Shaw) disclaim the pursuit of absolute truths, they seek to uncover (see below) a center to Stanley's personality that will explain his "reactions to the events of his experience."

Problems with the Classic, Objective Approach:
The Jack-Roller

The classic natural history approach fails to make problematic the set of issues considered in the last two chapters. It is a logocentric project. It seeks to find reason and order in lives. It views lives as rational constructions. It sees in a life materials for the testing and development of scientific hypotheses about human behavior. Turning lives into objects of study, this approach gives scant attention to the problems involved in describing real lives with real, objective meanings. While announcing a concern for the differences between objective experiences and their subjective, interactional meanings and expressions, the approach tells us surprisingly little about the gaps between experiences and their expressions. Indeed, practitioners like Shaw and Burgess escape into the "definition of the situation" dictum, when confronted with these gaps. Dancing around the problems of truthfulness and verifiable statements, these authors, committed as they are to the canons of positivist science, ignore the pervasive grey area that joins their life histories with narratives and fiction. Seeing themselves creating and contributing to a genre, they fail to see how the very conventions they are ascribing create the product they wish to analyze. They then proceed to assume the existence of knowledgeable authors, objective texts, starting points in lives, and the presence of influential others.

The classic stance pits the sociologist against the subject; it turns the subject into an object of study. It involves the production of a text that locates the subject inside a world that has been rendered understandable from the sociological point of view. Thus, both Shaw and Ernest W. Burgess (1930/1966, pp. 184-197), who discussed Stanley's case, attempted to explain why this particular youth became a juvenile delinquent.

Burgess, based on his reading of this and other life stories, was led to conclude that the personality is fixed in a child's early years. He argued that there are four personality types: (1) persons who view their lives in conventional terms, or Chroniclers; (2) Self-defenders, who justify their lives; (3) Confessants, who tell everything about themselves; and (4) Self-analysts, who analyze everything (Burgess, 1930/1966, p. 190).

Stanley, according to Burgess, was a self-defender. Hence, his story was full of rationalizations explaining why he became delinquent. Still, Burgess (and Shaw) felt that Stanley had no choice but to become delinquent. He came from a broken home and from an area of Chicago where delinquency was high. Moreover, Stanley's personality evidenced a series of traits which set him on the path of delinquency. These traits included self-pity, hypercriticalness of others, excessive interest in attention, ideas of persecution, always being right, blaming others, lack of self-insight, being suspicious of others, resentments, and the tendency to moralize (Burgess, 1930/1966, pp. 190-191). Burgess (1930/1966, p. 191) suggested that Stanley's personality traits were the

characteristic attributes of the personality pattern of the individual who is able even under the most adverse circumstances to maintain his ego against an unfriendly and even hostile social world.

Shaw and Burgess read these traits off of and from the text of Stanley's life. They saw Stanley as a person who imposed himself on others as a way of dealing with his humiliating life situations. They found a center to Stanley's life: his personality type.

In 1982, Jon Snodgrass found these same traits still present in Stanley, who, at the age of 69 in 1976, agreed to do a follow-up to his life story. Commenting on Stanley, who died in 1982 at the age of 75, Snodgrass observes:

I have tried to outline a pattern in Stanley's behavior; that is in order to avoid feelings of inferiority he repeatedly reacts by attempting to impress his superiority on others. . . . Burgess's identification of 'the early rise and persistence of a sense of injustice,' as a 'key' personality trait, is related to this theme (Snodgrass, 1982, p. 170).

Stanley found these same traits in himself (Snodgrass, 1982, p. 171), although at the time of his death he felt that he had overcome them (Snodgrass, 1982, p. 173). Here the subject merges with the social scientist. Stanley became the man Shaw said he would be, and this man, at the age of 75, told yet another social scientist that:

if anyone ever had an influence over me it was Shaw. . . . He would laugh at me, you see . . . I would be inclined to say, 'Who the hell is that guy, I'd like to punch him in the nose' (Snodgrass, 1982, p. 171).

And, a few months before he died, this man stated, "I am pleased also, if by this publication, I am helpful to Jon Snodgrass, his associates, and to social science" (Snodgrass, 1982, p. 173). Stanley, the man who made, after Wladek Wisniewski, the life history (and Clifford R. Shaw) famous in sociology, thanks sociology for having made him. This is what the classic natural history approach to life stories accomplished. It gave delinquents, prostitutes, alcoholics, drug addicts, and immigrants traits, personalities, personality flaws, and chances to tell their stories. It transformed subjects into sociology's images of who they should be. I turn now to the second variant within the objective approach, what is called the *objective hermeneutic* perspective.

Objective Hermeneutics and Biographical Narratives

The German sociologists Kohli (1981, 1986, 1987), Helling (1984, 1987, 1988), Schutze (1983), and Reimann and Schutze (1987) have offered the most advanced sociological developments of the objective approach. It has been given, although with qualifications (Helling, 1988, pp. 233-234), the label "objective hermeneutics"[2] by Oevermann's group in the following passage:

This method . . . when applied to the analysis of biographies, proceeds in the following way. First, all sociologically relevant information about the subject's course of life . . . is extracted from the account. The research team then constructs a typical course of life and typical hypothetical motivations of actions which could plausibly belong to a person of the extracted social attributes. [This] ... motivational structure is confronted with the actual information given by the respondent. The deviations of the individual case from the plausible case are used as a key to the structure of the individual case.

Helling goes on to note that this form of autobiography attempts to make interpretation a controllable activity. The unmistakable presence of Weber and Schutz is evident in the above passage, for the thrust is toward the construction of ideal-typical interpretations of meaningful experiences.

Many German biographical researchers object to the narrowness of Oevermann's project (Kohli, 1986, p. 106; Helling, 1988, pp. 222-240) and follow instead the leads of Schutze (1983) who has developed a method involving the narrative interview which merges the objective features of a subject's life with the subjective meanings attached to life experiences. This approach combines narrative interviewing, elements of "objective hermeneutics," and the grounded-theory approach to sampling and theory building developed by Glaser and Strauss (1967), and Strauss (1987).

This work retains a commitment to the development of qualitative counterparts to the usual criteria of validity, reliability, generalizability, and hypothesis testing, which have dominated in quantitative survey research. This leads to considerations of how subjects are sampled (theoretically, statistically), how representative they are, and to which populations generalizations can be applied (Helling, 1988, pp. 217-220). Such research is often driven by a set of hypotheses, i.e. how unemployment affects self-conception. In this sense, biographical information is used as a means of answering established sociological questions (Helling, 1988, p. 214). Issues of truth and objectivity are referred back to the ethnomethodological view of data being the product of social interaction. Truth is replaced by the concept of authenticity. Objectivity is used to refer to features of a subject's world which cannot be changed (Helling, 1988, p. 228). The validity and adequacy of an analysis is assessed in terms of the researcher's ability to account for and explain how a subject's definitions "are produced. . . . For this task she/he needs data other than the subject's knowledge, for which therefore the respondent cannot be used as an expert" (Helling, 1988, p. 232). This group has no analogue for the statistical concept of reliability, although one is sought (Helling, 1988, p. 232). On this and the related points concerning assessment, Helling (1988, p. 235-236) states:

> We have to develop criteria for the assessment of our work . . . we should not accept the criteria of survey research . . . but we should develop "qualitative analogues." . . . for every single biographical text, researchers must be able to show why they interpret it in a certain way . . . I do not believe that biographical texts speak for themselves. . . . Precisely because any text can be read in different ways, it must be established that a particular interpretation is valid.

Interpretive Strategies

This type of research is characterized by the following features. Investigators begin with an objective set of experiences in the subject's life. These are often connected to life-course stages (childhood, adolescence, early adulthood, old age) and to life-course experiences (i.e. education, marriage, employment). Concrete, contextual biographical materials are gathered via the use of the narrative interviewing strategy which involves a subject responding to a stimulus, i.e. recounting a set of life experiences in the form of a story or narrative. Interviewers then prompt subjects to expand on various sections of their stories. Respondents are next asked to theorize about their lives. The research group then subjects these narratives to careful readings and interpretations. Narrative segments and categories within the interview-story are isolated. Patterns of meaning and experience are sought. In this stage, the individual's biography is reconstructed and the structural-objective factors that have shaped his or her life are identified. An analytic abstraction of the case is written. This abstraction focuses on (1) the structural processes in the subject's life, (2) the different kinds of theories that relate to these life experiences, and (3) the unique and general features of the life. When the research group has finished the analysis of a single case, a second case is selected. The analysis of this case follows the same steps used in the interpretation of the first case. When this case analysis has been completed, the researchers formulate comparisons between cases. Theoretical generalizations are then developed which may emphasize any of the following: (1) career models, (2) structural processes in the life course, (3) models of social worlds, (4) relational models of biography, (5) natural history models of the life course (Reimann and Schutze (1987, pp. 64-66).

This "'new' life history [approach] is presently very much a method in the making" (Helling, 1988, p. 212). Its intent, as summarized by Helling and Reimann and Schutze, is to bring the classic life history approach in line with recent developments in ethnomethodology, socio-linguistics, and narrative analysis. It joins biographical experiences with sequences of objectively determined social-structural processes. Grounded theory seems to be the goal.

This work has several virtues. As just noted, it grasps the fundamental point that interview data, the hallmark of the classic life history, are interactional, contextual productions. There is a basic recognition that the interview text "is an interactive product, even before it is read and analyzed" (Helling, 1988, p. 235). Interviews are turned into occasions for storytelling, thus the narrative foundations of the life story are present from the beginning of the research. The research is triangulated; multiple perspectives on the same life experiences are sought. Each case is treated as a totality, as a universal singular. There is an attempt to extract multiple meanings from the stories. This involves a careful working back and forth between each element of the life to the broader, larger life picture.

This body of work has several disadvantages. Despite Helling's disclaimers about the implicit, quantitative thrust of the concerns for reliability and validity, the "new" life history approach belies a commitment to the biases of the classic, objective approach which reduced human experiences to data. While there is a concern for how the narrative text of an interview is produced, these researchers still assume that their texts capture the lives in question. A deconstructive reading of their project would focus on how they turn their subject's stories into data.

A linear model of biography is implied. This is not the simplistic model of the classic biographical approach. It is more complicated, for it is understood that there is never a perfect "correlation between the sequence of events judged as relevant by the researcher . . . called 'objective career points' and the subject's experience of them" (Helling, 1988, p. 239). Still, the subject is guided into a particular set of life experiences which are then discussed. This means that the researcher shapes the stories that are told. Even when efforts are made not to direct the subject, a linear model is still implied. Helling (1988, p. 240) sees the problem here:

narrative texts . . . 'freeze' events and 'lived experiences' into a rigid sequence, which suggests causality. Ambiguities and possibilities which belonged to life situations disappear in the 'A then B then C' structure of the narrative. Therefore, lived experience cannot be had; experience molded in a certain format can.

As Helling notes, lived experiences disappear from these interview-narratives, or they are frozen into static, rigid "A then B then C" format. Even though there is a recognition that analysts create meaning, how these meanings are produced in the readings of the stories is not clarified. The preoccupation with theory elevates the researcher's inter-pretations above the subject's. It makes this project basically a theory-driven endeavor. Even though this "new" approach parts company with the classic school, in the end it returns to a commitment to the objective view of life histories and life stories (Denzin, 1989b, p. 196). The interpretive writing style of this group objectifies the subject's life and, in the process, diminishes the subjective meanings of that life (Denzin, 1989b, p. 197). That is, the documentary evidence they use, which involves transcribed interviews, is no longer "the actual remains of something that once appeared in the actual world" (Goffman, 1974, p. 69). Narrative texts are interpreted as documentary evidence of real life experiences (Denzin, 1989b, p. 197). But they are not those expe-riences. They are something else, and that something else is not what they take it to be.

Interpretive Formats

Interpretive formats typically take one of three forms. First, there are those which are presented totally from the subject's point of view, without interpretation by the researcher (Lewis, 1970). Second are those approaches which rely upon the subject's perspective and are often written by the subject but are then used for sociological, psycho-logical, or anthropological interpretive purposes. (Sloan, 1987; Plum-mer, 1983). The social scientist interprets what the subject says. These interpretive approaches often blur with the "new" life history works discussed above. Third, there are those strategies which weave the subject's life into and through the researcher's interpretations of that life. Here the intent is to make sense of the life, but not for sociological or anthropological reasons (Sartre, 1971/1981). I will give these three forms the following names: (1) from the subject's point of view, (2) subject-produced autobiographies, and (3) making sense of an individual's life. I will briefly discuss each.

FROM THE SUBJECT'S POINT OF VIEW

Under this category fall the classic studies by Oscar Lewis (*La Vida,* 1969, *The Children of Sanchez,* 1970) which rest on the edited transcripts of informants' narratives. The resulting books have the flavor of literary productions.[3] While the invisible hand of Lewis is everywhere present in the text, the narratives are presented without interpretation. This format argues that a culture can be best understood by seeing its impact on the individual lives of family members. It works outward from a social collectivity, typically a family, to the larger social structure which shapes the lives of the members of the culture. Such documents can then be used as platforms for the expression of political positions (Lewis, 1970, p. 31).

Lewis's work was criticized because of his editing strategies and because of the vague, underlying culture-of-poverty theory that organized his larger project (Camargo, 1985, p. 42). Yet, his books stand as monuments to how the subject's voice can be captured and presented in "lifelike" fashion. Subject-interpreted lived-experience fills the pages of his books.

SUBJECT-PRODUCED AUTOBIOGRAPHIES

Consider the following statement. It is given by a thirty-five-year-old Finnish civil servant.

> There is nothing special to tell about in my life, on the contrary I feel that it has been most ordinary. This is thus not only my life, but it is a simplified description of several other women like me. My life has coincided with many changes in a society in the process of urbanization. I was born in the years of scarcity after the war. . . . I went to grammar schools . . . I came to Helsinki when 20 years old. . . . I studied . . . in the Helsinki School of Economics when women started studying there in numbers . . . I . . . had to look for a job at a time when my degree seems to have suffered from inflation . . . I have to confess that I was a loser from the beginning (Roos, 1987, pp. 15-16).

It took this woman seven years to find her current position of employment (Roos, 1987, p. 15).

This story was one of 300 autobiographies written by Finnish middle class employees in 1985 as part of a national competition. Participants were asked to "simply . . . write their autobiographies: no specific requirements or directives were given" (Roos, 1987, p. 8). The writers were asked to sign a waiver allowing their statements to be used for research and for subsequent publication. Writing autobiographies and taking part in national competitions is a common practice not only in Finland, but also in Poland, Iceland, and other Eastern European and Scandinavian countries. As Bertaux (1987, p. 3) notes, there is "the great Polish tradition of *pametniki*, public autobiographical competitions." This tradition may be traced back to Znaniecki and *The Polish Peasant.*

Several points need to be drawn from this public tradition of writing self-autobiographies. First, citizens in Finland, Iceland, Poland, and other Eastern European countries are able, without guidance, to produce these texts. The genre exists as a public form of self-expression. Second, the genre appears to be guided and structured by a body of taken-for-granted assumptions concerning how a life is to be represented, i.e. family, educational, and work history. Third, writers appear to be able to reflectively capture key moments in their own lives and give these moments personal and sociological meaning.[4] Fourth, these stories appear to express common narrative themes concerning the author as a person

> who has been put down, who is uncertain, does not believe in him [her]-self, thinks of him [her]-self as worthless in the eyes of others but has a terrible urge to become something, to show that this is not true (Roos, 1987, p. 7).

These writers express a form of biographical consciousness which reflects how difficult it is "to build a life history with a purpose, a sense of worth" (Roos, 1987, p. 7). Yet, there is a desire to do so, and this desire is realized by "a minor excuse, such as a competition" (Roos, 1987, p. 7).

Roos's reading of the above autobiography and two others leads him to argue that the realities of the new middle classes in Finland

> remain somewhat of an enigma . . . the autobiographies seem to show that this reality is in fact a very thin layer, under which a completely different world is revealed. The impact of this inner world is strong and lasting,

and makes the new middle classes seem more or less like a hastily constructed facade (Roos, 1987, p. 19).

Here the researcher uses the subject's life history as a vehicle for sociological theory. The self-autobiography is read as an instance of life in the new middle classes in Finland. A single case is used to represent a social class. The sociologist reasons from the particular to the general, treating each case as a universal singular. The story is accepted on face value. There is no preoccupation with its validity, accuracy, or authenticity, as there is for the other "new" life history researchers. Nor is there any attempt to cross-validate the story by collecting accounts from other persons in the subject's life, as there was for the "classic" researchers. The biographical texts that are studied are not, in any direct way, shaped by the presence of the sociologist's hand. These characteristics distinguish the "new" sociological interpreters from their earlier counterparts.

The Biographical Illusion

These differences between the new and the classic interpreters are further elaborated in the concerns of Roos and others for what is termed the *biographical illusion* (Bourdieu, 1986; Bertaux, 1987). Roos (1987, p. 17) discusses this concept in the following passage where he cites Pierre Bourdieu (1986) who states that:

> the joint interest of the object (the person himself) and subject (the researcher getting the story) of the biography project is to construct a coherent story, with a purpose . . . is an illusion . . . [for] in reality a biography is almost always a discontinuous story which lacks coherence in itself.

Bourdieu compares a life to a subway line "where the stops have no meanings by themselves, only as parts of a larger structure" (Roos, 1987, p. 17). Within this framework, the biographical project is an illusion, for any coherence that a life has is imposed by the larger culture, by the researcher, and by the subject's belief that his or her life should have coherence. Such a position is consistent with Bourdieu's general structural position which denies the presence and importance of the subject in both theory and everyday life.

Roos departs from Bourdieu on the following important points.[5] First, there are two logics which organize a life story or life history. The first is the logic of the social field, or the larger society and culture where a life is played out. In this social field, the subject may be positioned as an alienated worker, an unemployed female, or a divorced woman. This field will attach a range of meanings to the individuals who inhabit these positions. It will interpellate, or create a body of subjectivities for them. Second, there is the logic of the personal life of the individual who writes his or her life story. This logic may lead persons to believe that they have no control over their life, that they are worthless, or that they do have control and that they are worth something. These two logics may not overlap or coincide. Bourdieu calls these the external and internal logics of a story. When these two logics intersect, the biographical illusion, according to Bourdieu, exists. For example, the divorced, unemployed woman may feel stigmatized and worthless, and her life story will express self feelings.

However, as Roos (1987, p. 17) argues, when these logics do not overlap, it becomes more difficult to sustain the argument that biographical coherence is an illusion. Furthermore, and this is Roos's second point, from whose point of view is the illusion seen? If the subject sees coherence and the researcher doesn't, who is correct? At what moment in time is the illusion established? Bourdieu's arguments concerning biographical coherence are important. A similar argument was made in chapter 1. However, as argued in chapter 2 in the discussion of experience and its expression, reading an overlap between two fields of experience (the social and the personal) is difficult and involves an imposition of one interpretive frame (the researcher's) on another. Once again, the sociological subject is turned into an object of sociological theorizing.

The point to make is not whether biographical coherence is an illusion or a reality. Rather, what must be established is how individuals give coherence to their lives when they write or talk self-autobiographies. The sources of this coherence, the narratives that lie behind them, and the larger ideologies that structure them must be uncovered.[6] Bourdieu's general position glosses the complexities of this process.

Making Experience Come Out Right

The anthropologist David W. Plath (1987), in an article with the title, "Making Experience Come Out Right: Culture as Biography," thickens Bourdieu's illusion by showing how culture and cultural meanings are not external to the life and meanings of the self but constitutive of it. A careful and detailed reading of Montaigne's *Essays* (1572-1588/1958) leads Plath to propose that the autobiographical meanings of the self are fundamentally unstable and realized only through time and temporality. Montaigne's self is "consubstantial" with his writings. He wrote himself into his essays. He says of his writings:

> In modeling this figure upon myself, I have had to fashion and compose myself so often to bring myself out, that the model itself has to some extent grown firm and taken shape. Painting myself for others, I have painted my inward self with colors clearer than my original ones. I have no more made my book than my book has made me—a book consubstantial with its author, concerned with my own self, an integral part of my life (Montaigne, 1958, p. 504, quoted by Plath, 1987, p. 3).

Each time Montaigne writes himself into his text, he creates a new picture of who he is. He is who he writes, and who he writes keeps changing. His self is a temporal production. He is not a biographical illusion, he is a biographical production. He is attempting to capture his deep, inner, inward self, understanding that he is more than his words make him out to be. His selfhood, as evidenced in his autobiographical writings, can only be understood as a temporal phenomenon, "and not as a 'structure' individuated and spaced-out from the rest of culture. Culture . . . becomes a window-of-opportunity for the completing of self-projects" (Plath, 1987, p. 1). In this view, Bourdieu's position can be seen as making culture a structure which creates biographies and selves. Plath's position challenges this interpretation and directs our attention, as indicated above, to how persons create and give meaning to their lives in the autobiographical texts they produce. This temporal process will make the self consubstantial with the artifacts the culture makes available to the person. At the same time, the person may be seen as creating artifacts like autobiographies, which are, for them, consubstantial with who they are.

Group Storytelling

An important variation on subject-produced autobiographies is the method of having subjects in groups develop their own versions of their life histories. McCall (1985, 1989) created storytelling groups of persons born in the 1940s. She met with these groups weekly over a several month period. Group participants were given assignments to write stories about a variety of different topics or events in their lives, including their marriages, their work, their divorces, their first dates, the birth of their children, and so on. A recurring theme of the stories dealt with the changing American family and the place of these individuals, as single parents, in this institution.

Jean Richards, married in 1961 and divorced in 1974, comments on the problems in her life:

> Ending a marriage and beginning an education, I literally bit off more than I could chew. I lost weight, developed ulcers, became temperamental. . . . I asked all the questions. . . . How would I make the house payments? Where would I get the money for food and clothes? . . . What about Christmas? Who can I turn to? (McCall and Wittner, 1988, p. 13).

McCall observes that, "Reading their stories aloud and discussing them, members of these storytelling groups also created new shared understandings of their lives and their life problems they shared" (McCall and Wittner, 1988, p. 14). Her research shows how ordinary people "create culture when they tell stories" (McCall and Wittner, 1988, p. 14). To borrow Plath's phrase, the selves of these ordinary people become consubstantial with the stories they told one another. Not only did they create culture, but they created and re-created themselves in the process.

Making Sense of an Individual's Life I: Sartre and Flaubert

Those interpretive projects which attempt to make sense of the subject's life typically, like Sartre (1971/1981), take a subject's works as the beginning point of inquiry. They then attempt to interpret who the subject is by reading through those productions. It is assumed that the "real" subject will be found in these documents. Sartre (1971/1981, p. x) phrases this assumption in the following words. He is discussing Flaubert:

> he is objectified in his books. Anyone will tell you, 'Gustave Flaubert — he's the author of *Madame Bovary.*' What then is the relationship of the man to the work?

If Flaubert is objectified in his works, Sartre finds a part of himself in Flaubert. He states: "Why Flaubert? For three reasons. The first, very personal . . . in 1943, rereading his correspondence. . . . I felt I had a score to settle with Flaubert and ought to get to know him better" (Sartre, 1971/1981, p. x).

Sartre's project, then, is an attempt to get to know Flaubert better as he attempts to answer the question, "What can we know about a man?" To know a man, Sartre is led to reread all of Flaubert's works, letters, diaries, autobiographies, letters written to him, and accounts others gave of him. He then organizes his study in terms of the following topics: (1) a problem, (2) the father, (3) the mother, (4) the elder brother, (5) the birth of a younger son, (6) father and son, (7) two ideologies, (8) the imaginary child, (9) from imaginary child to actor, (10) from actor to author, (11) scripta mament, and (121) from poet to artist.

Four assumptions organize Sartre's attempts to understand Flaubert. The first involves where to begin the study. Sartre (1971/1981, p. x) observes:

> Now we must begin. How, and by what means? It doesn't much matter: a corpse is open to all comers. The essential thing is to set out with a problem. The one I have chosen is hardly ever discussed. Let me read this passage from a letter. . . . 'It is by the sheer force of work that I am able to silence my innate melancholy. But the old nature often reappears, the old nature that no one knows, the deep, always hidden wound.' What is the meaning of this? Can a wound be innate? In any event Flaubert refers us to his prehistory . . . we must try to understand . . . the origin of the wound that is 'always hidden' and dates back to his earliest childhood. That will not, I think, be a bad start.

Here Sartre exposes his commitment to the view that all life histories have their origins in early childhood. This is his first assumption. The story must begin with the individual's prehistory. His second assumption argues that in this prehistory there will be an event that indelibly shapes the life of the person. For Flaubert, it is a deep, early wound that involved his late entry into language. Sartre's third assumption is evident in the organization of his two-volume work on Flaubert. As noted above, his choice and ordering of topics take Flaubert from childhood through adulthood. They turn on the influences of first the father, then the mother, then siblings, then the relation between the father and the son, then early ventures into being an actor and an author. Sartre sees Flaubert's life unfolding through a series and sequences of stages which double back on one another as Flaubert struggles to discover who he is.

Sartre's fourth assumption involves the problems of telling when Flaubert is telling the truth about his life. He argues (1971/1981, p. 182): "We have found that Gustave, whenever he writes in the first person, is insincere. . . . But he gives himself up when he invents." When Flaubert exaggerates, his "fiction permits him to say what he feels . . . lying . . . cheats us by truth" (Sartre, 1971/1981, p. 188). Sartre reads many of Flaubert's so-called factual accounts of his life as inventions, often "curious and deceitful text[s] . . . the rule is strict" (Sartre, 1971/1981, pp. 7, 9). In short, what Flaubert says about his life is not to be trusted. What he writes in his fiction is to be taken as truthful. Thus Sartre assumes that there are facts, facticities, and fictions about Flaubert and his life. There are at least two Flauberts: the man who fabricated events and experiences about his "real" life and the man who wrote himself into his fiction. The "real" Flaubert is to be found in the fictions he wrote. Sartre locates truth in fiction.

Such a position presumes that the "real" facts and facticities about a life can be discovered. It assumes the presence in fiction of an intentional author whose real meanings can be ascertained. That Flaubert went to such lengths to disguise himself and to misrepresent his experiences should alert us to the fact that he doubted his own intentionality. Like Montaigne, he sought the consubstantiality of himself in his works; and they were all fictions.

Sartre found the Flaubert he wanted to find by positing a "real" subject who lurked inside his so-called "fictional" texts. But this distinction between Flaubert's two texts, his first person accounts and his fictions, cannot be allowed.[7] All of Flaubert's writings were fiction. There were (and are) only multiple versions of his subjectivity.

Making Sense of an Individual's Life II: Alcoholics

I turn now to a brief discussion of a variant on Sartre's approach to making sense of an individual's life. Like Sartre, this variant assumes the existence of a pivotal event in a person's life. It also assumes that this event will be a pivotal meaning structure that organizes the other activities in a person's life. This strategy involves studying how this event comes to occupy a central place in a person's life. It then examines how the meanings of this event change over time. It attempts to anchor the meanings of this event in larger cultural settings, including the mass media, the popular culture, and interacting groups.

I employed this approach in my study of American alcoholics (Denzin, 1987a, 1987b, 1986b). The pivotal meaning structure for the active alcoholic involves drinking and those social acts that connect the person to alcohol. The pivotal meaning structure for the recovering alcoholic involves not drinking, or abstinence from alcohol. Alcoholics Anonymous (A.A.) replaces alcohol in the lives of many recovering alcoholics.

The Progressive-Regressive Method

In order to study these meaning structures, I listened to the self stories alcoholics told one another around the A.A. meeting tables. From these stories, I worked back in biographical time to discover how the individual first became a drinker, than an alcoholic drinker, and than a recovering alcoholic who no longer drank. The author employed a variant of Sartre's (1963, pp. 85-166) progressive-regressive method which begins with a key event in a subject's live and then works forward and backward from that event. In my study, forward progression began with the individual's participation in A.A. and admission of his or her alcoholism. I listened to these individuals as they began to discuss their past life experiences. I worked backward, identifying how the person got to A.A. in the first place.

I then employed three interpretive strategies adopted from Paul Thompson's (1978) treatment of oral history materials. First, I collected single life-story, life-history narratives involving a select number of "oldtimers" in the A.A. groups I studied. Second, I collected self stories organized around single themes, like relapses, treatment experiences, marriages and divorces, first getting to A.A., and so on. Third, I did a cross-build, an interpretive account of how individuals became confirmed A.A. members and recovering alcoholics.

My intentions were not to unravel lives, find the real meanings of lives, or discover who the "real" alcoholic was. Rather, I examined how alcoholics represented themselves to one another in the A.A. setting through the stories they told one another. I assumed, however, that uncovering the meanings to the pivotal event in their lives was a key to understanding how they became recovering alcoholics. In these senses, I stayed within the framework of Sartre's project but departed from it because I made no attempt to probe the prehistory of the A.A. members. Nor did I attempt to discover the "real" person behind the A.A. stories that were told. I did assume, however, that the deep, inner selves of the individuals he studied were revealed in the stories he listened to.

Conclusions

I have examined several different formats for reading lives, starting with the classic, objective, natural history approach and its contemporary, objective, hermeneutic variations. Three more purely interpretive frameworks were then discussed: those organized strictly from the subject's point of view—self-autobiographies written by subjects, group self-stories, and two projects which focused on making sense of an individual's life. The problems of the biographical illusion, and biographical coherence were again taken up. In the next chapter I will discuss problems involved in reading lived experiences and treating these experiences as biographical material. I will be focusing on epiphanies, or turning-point moments in person's lives, self stories, and personal experience stories.

NOTES

1. See Helling, 1987 and 1988, and Kohli, 1986 for reviews.
2. Hermeneutics refers to the process or act of interpretation. Presumably, "objective" hermeneutics means objective interpretation, whatever that means.
3. See Camargo, 1985 for a discussion of Lewis's project and a review of how this method is currently being used in Latin America.
4. See McCall, 1989 for another example of this general point.
5. See also Bertaux's discussion of Bourdieu, 1987, pp. 47-50.
6. See Denzin, 1987b, pp. 190-193 for a discussion of how this works for recovering alcoholics.
7. The writings about the life of the playwright Lillian Hellman provide another illustration of this futile attempt to locate the "true" facts about an author (see Hellman, 1970, 1973, 1976; Feibleman, 1988; Rollyson, 1988; Wright, 1986; Kanfer, 1988). Hellman was called "one of the most adventurous and tough-minded playwrights in the history of American theater" (Jane Fonda), a fraud, an "artist of veneer-deep authenticity" (Mary McCarthy), "a mother, a sister, and a friend" (William Styron), "someone who displayed a high finish of integrity, decency and uprightness" (John Hersey), a woman "who could upstage God" (Peter Feibleman). About her writing, Mary McCarthy stated "Every word she writes is a lie, including 'and' and 'the' (Kanfer, 1988, p. 15). By taking the position that truth and fiction are separate productions, the writings on and about Hellman ignore the fact that all of her statements were fictions. The "true" story of Hellman can never be produced.

4. SELVES, STORIES, AND EXPERIENCES

In earlier chapters, I defined the biographical method as the studied use and collection of life documents that describe turning-point moments in an individual's life. It remains to examine how these moments are studied, understanding that only the representations of experience can ever be captured. Accordingly, my topic in this chapter is reading the traces and evidences of problematic experience that are given in those personal-experience self-stories. I will offer a discussion of the epiphany and then discuss how it is possible to make sense of these experiences and their expressions. This is intended as an applications or example chapter which puts into place the definitional and assumption-listing work of chapters 1 to 3. I will conclude with a short discussion of obituaries, indicating how stories never stay closed. But first, a brief aside on the importance of studying problematic, lived experiences, and then an example.

Capturing and Studying Lived Experience

In the last chapter, it was argued that narrative texts, like the kind Helling and her colleagues collect, freeze events and lived experiences into rigid sequences (Helling, 1988, p. 240). The ambiguities and complexities of life situations thus seldom appear in the analyst's text. The corpus of experience disappears into a text that is then read as a representation of the life experiences of the individual being studied. There are no experiences, only glossed, narrative reports of them. The use and the value of the biographical method lies in its user's ability to capture, probe, and render understandable problematic experience. If this cannot be done, if subject representations of lived experiences, as given in stories, cannot be captured, then the method ends up producing the kinds of documents I have continually criticized in the preceding chapters. It is necessary to get as close to actual experience as possible.[1] Now, an example.

BILLS' STORY

Consider the following self story. The speaker is a thirty-year-old white male, an engineer, single, sober six years in Alcoholics Anonymous. He is telling a version of his life story to an "open" A.A. meeting. The focus of such stories is specified in A.A.'s *Big Book, Alcoholics Anonymous* (1976, p. 58): "Our stories disclose in a general way what we used to be like, what happened, and what we are like now." The story begins:

> "My name's Bill and I'm an alcoholic. I became an alcoholic at about the age of 16. I learned to drink when I was a sophomore in high school with my friends. We would steal booze from my parent's liquor cabinet. We started drinking before classes started at school. Later I learned how to buy friends with my parent's booze. I had a girl friend for 8 years. We used to drink together and mess around. Then I lost her. I started drifting after high school. Everybody did. I became a hippie. It was the thing to do. Went to a commune in Oregon and learned how to catch salmon. Took every drug anybody ever took. Built a cabin in the woods and I guess I found God. Anyway I thought he spoke to me. I came back home and decided to just drink beer. I wasn't working. Every day I would go to Al's Pub at 3:00 p.m. and sit in the same chair. But before I went to the Pub I stopped at the bank, it was right around the corner. I'd cash a check, this was everyday, for $7.75. Now there's a story behind this which I don't have time to tell you. But anyway, you see I was afraid to make change at the bar. So with $7.75 I had money for three pitchers of beer ($2.00 a piece), .75 for cigarettes, they hadn't gone up yet, and four quarters to play the juke box. I'd sit there until I got good and drunk and then I'd go home and pass out. This went on for three years. $7.75 everyday, same bar stool, same three pitchers of beer, same music on the juke box. It got worse. I started seeing things. I ended up in the mental health clinic. Thirty days. Somebody from A.A. came and saw me. I got out, started going to meetings and still drinking. One night I went to my psychiatrist and he told me to stop drinking. I did. I haven't had a drink since that night. I go to 5 meetings a week. I go to Al-Anon. I'm very close to my family. My life has gotten better. Thank you for letting me talk."

I will return to this story in a moment.

The Epiphany

Epiphanies are interactional moments and experiences which leave marks on people's lives (Denzin, 1989a, chapters 1 and 7). In them, personal character is manifested. They are often moments of crisis. They alter the fundamental meaning structures in a person's life. Their effects may be positive or negative. They are like Victor Turner's (1986, p. 41) "liminal phase of experience." In the liminal, or threshold, moment of experience, the person is in a "no-man's land betwixt and between . . . the past and the . . . future" (Turner, 1986, p. 41). These are existential acts. Some are ritualized, as in status-passages; others are even routinized, as when a man daily batters and beats his wife. Still others are totally emergent and unstructured, and the person enters them with few if any prior understandings of what is going to happen. The meanings of these experiences are always given retrospectively, as they are relived and reexperienced in the stories persons tell about what has happened to them.

Forms of the Epiphany

Elsewhere (Denzin, 1989a, chapter 7) I distinguished four forms of the epiphany: (1) the *major event,* which touches every fabric of a person's life; (2) the cumulative or *representative event,* which signifies eruptions or reactions to experiences which have been going on for a long period of time; (3) the *minor epiphany,* which symbolically represents a major, problematic moment in a relationship or a person's life; and (4) those episodes whose meanings are given in the *reliving* of the experience. I called these, respectively, the major epiphany, the cumulative epiphany, the illuminative or minor epiphany, and the re-lived epiphany. (Several examples of each of these forms are given in Denzin, 1989a, chapter 7).

BILL'S STORY AGAIN

Return to Bill's story. It contains everything that is needed in order to achieve the goals of the biographical method as earlier defined. Each form of the epiphany is present. The major forms are seen in Bill's learning how to drink, his stopping drinking, seeing God, taking drugs, stealing from his parents, seeing things, going to the mental health clinic. The cumulative, representative, and minor epiphanies are evidenced in his daily trips to the bank and to Al's Pub. Day after day for three years, he repeated these experiences as he took his place on the same bar stool and played the same music. Retrospectively, he relives these experiences as he tells them to his A.A. audience. In this telling, he turns back on his life and brings it up to date. In order to make sense out of who Bill is today, we, as listeners, need to know these things about him.

His story as narrative is filled with multiple stories, stories within stories. Each story is organized in terms of an epiphanal moment. There is the story of how he learned to drink and get friends in high school. There are the stories of how he became a hippie, took drugs, built a cabin in the woods, saw God, and fished for salmon. There is the story, which he could tell but only alludes to, about his fear of making change at the bar, so he had to stop at the bank and cash a check for $7.75 everyday.

These are glossed, indexically understood stories which do not need to be elaborated. Their meanings are contextualized within the framework of the larger story he is telling. They are part of the performance that is called "telling one's story as an alcoholic at an open A.A. meeting." Hence, storytelling is a performative self-act carried out before a group of listeners. The self and personal-experience story is a story-for-a-group. It is a group story.

But more is involved. As Bill speaks, he throws his story out to the audience who hears it. This audience becomes part of the story that is told. A third structure emerges. Not only is Bill talking about his alcoholic self, but he is telling his stories to other alcoholic selves. A group self is formed; a self lodged and located in the performative occasion of the "open meeting."

A story that is told is never the same story that is heard. Each teller speaks from a biographical position that is unique and, in a sense, unshareable. Each hearer of a story hears from a similarly unshareable position. But these two versions of the story merge and run together into a collective, group version of the story that was told. Because there are always stories embedded within stories, including the told story and the heard story, there are only multiple versions of shareable and unshareable personal experiences.

When sociologists and other listeners seek to find a common ground of consensual meaning within a story or to establish common meanings that extend across stories, all they end up with are glossed, indexically meaningful, yet de-personalized versions of the life experiences they wish to understand. There is no warrant in such practices.

Stories within stories told to groups remind us that every life story is a multiplicity of stories that could be told. There is no single life story or self-autobiography that grasps or covers all that a life is for a person. There are only multiple stories that can be told. Each storyteller can only tell the stories his or her biography allows to be told. We are, as Heidegger (1962) reminds us, talking beings, and we live and talk our way into being through the poetic, narrative structures of our language. It's not that our language tells our stories for us; rather, we appropriate language for our own discursive purposes. This is what Bill has done.

A doubling of self occurs in Bill's story. He sees himself reflected in the stories he is telling. He becomes a second self within his story, for he is telling a story about himself. This second self is a temporal production, lodged in the past but told in the present. In this temporalizing process, multiple selves speak: the self of the storyteller, the self of the person who built a cabin in Oregon, the self of the recovering alcoholic telling a series of stories about himself, the self telling a story to an open A.A. meeting, and so on. These multiple selves merge, double back, laminate and build on one another, and provide the context and occasion for the production of the larger story that is told.

The boundaries and borders between the multiple stories is never clear-cut, for the meanings of every given story is only given in the difference that separates its beginnings and endings from the story that follows. As one story ends, another begins, but then the earlier story overlaps with the one that is now being told. Stories become arbitrary constructions within the larger narratives that contain the story the teller is attempting to tell.

Bill is producing an oral history, an oral text which is the text of his life at this moment in his personal history. As he does so, he locates himself within the oral, storytelling tradition of Western culture. His story follows the narrative outlines of the Western self as it has been reconstituted within the A.A. cultural texts: grace and innocence, fall from grace, and final redemption (Misch, 1951, Volume 1; Denzin, 1987b, pp. 169-170). His story is thus continuous with all those other stories that came before his.

The Cultural Locus of Stories

No self or personal-experience story is ever an individual production. It derives from larger group, cultural, ideological, and historical contexts. So it is with Bill's story. His story is located within A.A.'s cultural texts and in the shared history of the A.A. experience. To understand a life, the epiphanies and the personal-experience and self stories that represent and shape that life, one must penetrate and understand these larger structures. They provide the languages, emotions, ideologies, taken-for-granted understandings, and shared experiences from which the stories flow.

The alcoholic's stories emanate from three broad, group structures: the family, A.A., and the group before whom the story is told. For A.A. storytellers like Bill, the A.A. group and the A.A. cultural texts define the broad outlines of the self story. But behind every alcoholic stands a family and a structure of family experiences which have become part of his or her story. An unraveling of a story such as Bill's involves an unraveling of the family history that is part of his self.

The A.A. audience members who heard Bill's story had, on different occasions, learned the following facts about his family history: (1) his mother is a recovering alcoholic and a manic-depressive, as is Bill, who is on medication; (2) his father is an autocratic family patriarch; (3) his sister is a manic-depressive, employed as a social worker; (4) his brother is getting his Ph.D; (5) his mother fears for his sanity, fears that he will never complete his higher education program and get a job, feels that he doesn't know how to relate to women and, hence, will probably never get married.

With this knowledge in hand, the audience heard more of Bill's story then he told. They knew that the glossed family history briefly mentioned in his larger story contained references to his mother, brother, father, sister, and his own history of mental illness. These taken-for-granted understandings constituted a frame of reference for understanding the larger story that was told and heard. A culturally understood self, a self grounded in the culturally expected references to family, drinking, and recovery, was produced in and through Bills' talk. A sociological listener unfamiliar with these features of Bill's personal history would not have heard these things.

Limits of the Story

A story is always an interpretive account; but, of course, all interpretations are biased. However, many times a storyteller neglects important structural factors which have impinged on his or her life. Or, if such forces are addressed, they are interpreted from the teller's biased point of view. Many times a person will act as if he or she made his or her own history when, in fact, he or she was forced to make the history he or she lived (Denzin, 1986c). The following speaker does this:

"You know I made the last four months by myself. I haven't used or drank. I'm really proud of myself. I did it."

A friend, listening to this account commented:

"You know you were under a court order all last year. You didn't do this on your own. You were forced to, whether you want to accept this fact or not. You also went to A.A. and N.A. Listen Buster. You did what you did because you had help and because you were afraid and thought you had no other choice. Don't give me this, 'I did it on my own crap!'" (Denzin, 1986c, p. 334).

The speaker replies, "I know. I just don't like to admit it."

This listener invokes two structural forces, the state and A.A., which accounted in part for this speaker's experiences. To have secured only the speaker's account, without a knowledge of his biography and personal history, would have produced a biased interpretation of his situation.

Process, Structure, and Stories

The intent of the biographical project is to uncover the social, economic, cultural, structural, and historical forces that shape, distort, and otherwise alter problematic lived experiences (Bertaux, 1981b, p. 4). This focus on structure must never lose sight of the individuals who live these structurally shaped lives. On the other hand, subjectivity must not be romanticized.

Now consider another story. Gary, a self-defined addict and alcoholic, is speaking in a closed A.A. meeting, which means that only persons who call themselves alcoholics are present.

GARY'S STORY

"I've lied to you people for six months. I got drunk last night and used cocaine. I've been getting high every day that I've been coming here. I use cocaine in the morning, before I go to meetings and at night. I guess I'm an addict. When I told my story at the area breakfast (the same open meeting Bill told his story to), I neglected to say that I had been using cocaine everyday. I guess I was lying. . . . I think I need to get honest with myself. But I don't know how. I've lied to myself for so long I don't know what's true and what's false."

True and False Stories?

Gary's story brings us, once again, to the problems of truth and the accurate representations of a life and its experiences. By his own admission, he has been lying to the A.A. group for months. He has also been lying to himself. He would be the first person to say that he cannot tell the difference between what is a lie and what is the truth.

Several problems are at work in this account. The stories other alcoholics heard Gary tell were "heard-as-true-stories," although some listeners may have expected that he was lying. To tell a story that is heard as true, means that the speaker must know the group's criteria for what is true and what is false and know how to present a self that will be in conformity with the group's conceptions and standards of truthfulness. A story heard as true becomes part of the teller's public biography. Gary knew how to tell such a story. He was seen as having built up six months of "clean and sober" time. He was told by others that he was doing well; that he was making great strides in his program. As he heard these comments, he knew — or a part of him knew — that he was using cocaine and was not the "clean and sober" person he was presenting himself as being.

Knowing how a true story is told, Gary is now confronted with the problem of telling a story that truthfully states that he has been lying. He needs to tell a story that discounts the false stories he has been telling. In order to convince his listeners that he is now telling the truth, he has to convince them that he had earlier been telling lies. A false story can only be discredited by another story, which requires that it be heard as a true story. He does this by stating that he was using cocaine over the period of time he said that he was "clean and sober."

Assuming that Gary is now telling the truth, and assuming that the group assumes that he is now telling the truth, how do self-story researchers know when and if the stories they hear are true or false? Faulkner reminds the readers of his trilogy on the Snopes family that not even Flem Snopes told himself what he was up to. How do we know what we are up to when we are hearing stories told by persons who may not know what they are up to? This problem extends beyond the validity or the factual accuracy of a story. It involves processes that cut to the core of what it means to be a person who is able to tell stories about himself or herself.

Every storyteller has two options when telling a story: to tell a story that accords with the fictional facts about his or her life, or to tell a story which departs from those facticities. Sociologists as listeners are seldom in a position to tell the difference between these two narrative forms. This is acutely the case when the teller has learned the cultural ways of the social group from whose structures his or her story comes. Garfinkel learned this lesson in his study of Agnes.

Now Becker (1986, pp. 3, 280, and 294) reminds us that, "knowledge is relative . . . and *is* what I can get other people to accept . . . but that truth need not be the *whole* truth . . . [and] the question is whether . . . X *and only* X is true, or . . . that, while X is true, Y is too" (italics in original). Gary's stories were both true and false: he hadn't been drinking, except for the night before he told this story (true), but he had been using, when he said he had been clean and sober (false).

Many groups aren't as loose as Becker. They want truthful statements that apply to every instance of a phenomenon, not to just some of them. They want X and only X to be true, and not X and sometimes Y and then sometimes Z. In A.A., you are either "clean and sober" or you are not. So, while knowledge and truth are relative across groups and settings, within settings they often are not. Researchers must establish the criteria of truth that operate in the groups that are studied. It will be these criteria that structure the stories that are told by the group members.

Here is the dilemma. There are only interpretations, and all that people tell are self stories. The sociologist's task cannot be one of determining the difference between true and false stories. All stories, as argued earlier, are fictions. The sociologist's task, then, involves studying how persons and their groups culturally produce warrantable self and personal-experience stories which accord with that group's standards of truth.[2] We study how persons learn how to tell stories which match a group's understandings of what a story should look and sound like. It seems that little more can or needs to be said on this matter of truthfulness and knowing.

I have thus far attempted to establish the following points: (1) stories always come in multiple versions, and they never have clear endings or beginnings; (2) stories are grounded in a group's culture where criteria of truthfulness are established; (3) the stories told are never the same as the stories heard; (4) stories are shaped by larger ideological forces which put pressure on persons to establish their individuality (and self control) in the stories they construct.

I turn now to a narrative form which has some similarities to the diary, for it is an account that is meant for no one else. I call it the self-narrative.

The Self-Narrative

Like a diary entry, the following statement from Gary speaks to a private self. Such statements are sought because they remind us that there is always more to the self than is given in a story told in front of a group or given to an interviewer. Gary wrote the following lines the night before he entered a treatment center. I retain his spelling and punctuation.

"I have a lot of fear in me as you know i am shure afraid of getting close close to people and letting people get close to me this fear has hurt me more times than I care to think about. ifve tried to work on it but no luck i get close to it and i freak out and drink or drug its heart breaking to know that this hurts my life the way it does and it also hurts others to in my life that care and others tht have tried to care but backed off from me, that i can understand so it just snowballs and i hurt inside. ive really have never really forgotten my past . . . I just feel like this empty person just here and not doing anything else iam sad about this i just feel like crawling inside of a hole and staing there god help me please let me be a full person and let me love me so i can love others iam sick this way of thinking and living iam asking for help i can't go on like it anylonger iam at the turning point to want to change to live clean and sober i feel sick because iam sick inside, what happened to me?"

Gary is pouring out his inner self to himself. He seeks to inscribe the meanings of these words in the self that he lives. He reminds us that all we have, as Sartre wrote, are words. Our humanness and our selfness lie in the words we speak and attach to ourselves. These words, hollow, often empty, learned from others, spoken and written by us, are all that we have. To live their lives into the words that they speak is what all speakers are after. As students of the biographical method, we find, then, that all that we too have are words. Now what do we make of them? Perhaps, we, like Faulkner's Flem Snopes, don't even know what we are up to when we put words after one another and call the results of our efforts biographical analysis.

It seems fitting to end with obituaries, for, in these endings to lives, surely the final meanings of a person are found.

Obituaries

Here is how the *New York Times* (July 20, 1988, p. 50) reported the death of Martin J. Walsh:

Martin J. Walsh
Actor, 41
New York, July 19 — Martin J. Walsh, an actor died of acquired immune deficiency syndrome on July 7 at New York University Medical Center in Manhattan. He was 41 years old.

Mr. Walsh appeared in Broadway in "The Pirates of Penzance" and "Shenandoah" and many other Off Broadway productions. He was a member of The Prince Street Players, a children's theater company, in the 1970s.

He is survived by his father . . . a brother . . . and three sisters. . . .

The small number of lines given to Mr. Walsh and his death contrasts with the three column story, accompanied by a photograph, of Raymond Carver's death, reported in the same newspaper on Wednesday, August 3, 1988.

Like Mr. Walsh's life and death, Mr. Carver's life is recorded in terms of his work and the family he left behind. But Mr. Carver's biography is filled out. He is called a writer and poet of the working poor. Frog, his childhood nickname, is discussed, as are his collections of short stories, the awards he won, his early childhood, his marriages, his alcoholism, his divorce from his first wife, his operations for cancer, his relations to the poet Tess Gallagher, and his final moments alive on his porch looking at his rose garden while he talked about Chekov's death.

The obituary makes a public statement of a life's end. It represents a narrative form which goes from birth (the beginning), to death (the end). It gives a life a finite temporal space. It then fills out that space with the accomplishments of the person. It makes a life consubstantial with its achievements. When, as in the case of Mr. Carver, the life that was led was noteworthy, then personal words and personal experience stories from the dead individual's life are recorded. Unnoteworthy lives seldom get such coverage.

Are we to assume that Martin J. Walsh's life was any less significant than Raymond Carver's because less space was devoted to it? Surely not for his father, brother and three sisters. Both men suffered from social diseases: Walsh died from his, AIDS; Carver presumably recovered from his alcoholism. Both of these social diseases became part of the public biographies in their moment of death. The obituary seeks a cause for life's end, and it attempts to find in that cause an interpretation of the life that died from it. Whether the cause is AIDS, cancer, alcoholism, or old age, that cause, a marker of an ending, is read back into a life, showing that one final meaning of a life is always given in terms of its ending.

But even this search for final causes is itself open-ended, for the life that is inscribed in the obituary is presented as an on-going concern. Mr. Walsh's life goes on in the memories of his family, and Mr. Carver's life is similarly continued in his obituary; and he, like Mr. Walsh, lives on in his works. The obituary, then, is never a closed text, even though it presents itself as being one.

The obituary treats each individual as an universal singular and, in this literary move, it recognizes that each individual's life is itself a singular accomplishment which demands recognition. That achievement, summed up in the activities and experiences of the person, is all that the person is or ever was. This named entity, this person who is dead, is now brought before us in full biographical garb. Here in these bare details we find that all a life is, as far as the public is concerned, is what its owner did and who he or she leaves behind. A life, like the stories that can be told about it, never ends.

But there is more, and Gary tells us this in his private self-narrative. There is a deep, inner self groping for meaning, and this self and its meanings are forever and always unfinished productions. The biographical method is always incomplete, for the lives and experiences this method attempts to capture are themselves never done. Newspapers can't allow this, nor can sociologists. But some everyday, ordinary people and the people who write about them—like Raymond Carver—do.

NOTES

1. See Denzin, 1989a, chapter 2 for an extended discussion of how to do this.

2. As a group, students of biographies and autobiographies appear to have a set of criteria regarding truthfulness that is often not held by their subjects. This accounts, in part, for the continual preoccupation with this problem in the literature.

5. IN CONCLUSION: REPRESENTING LIVES
Pentimento: "Something painted
out of a picture which later
becomes visible again."

Lives and their experiences are represented in stories. They are like pictures that have been painted over, and, when paint is scraped off an old picture, something new becomes visible. What is new is what was previously covered up. A life and the stories about it have the qualities of *pentimento.* Something new is always coming into sight, displacing what was previously certain and seen. There is no truth in the painting of a life, only multiple images and traces of what has been, what could have been, and what now is.

These stories move outward from the selves of the person and inward to the groups that give them meaning and structure. Persons are arbitrators of their own presence in the world, and they should have the last word on this problem. Our texts must always return to and reflect the words persons speak as they attempt to give meaning and shape to the lives they lead. The materials of the biographical method resolve, in the final analysis, into the stories persons tell one another.

These stories are learned and told in cultural groups. The stories that members of groups pass on to one another are reflective of understandings and practices that are at work in the larger system of cultural understandings that are acted upon by group members. These understandings contain conceptions of persons' lives, meaningful, subjective experience, and notions of how persons and their experiences are to be represented. There are only stories to be told and listened to. These stories resolve the dilemmas surrounding the metaphysics of presence that haunts the individual as he or she attempts to give shape to this thing called a life and a biography. One becomes the stories one tells. The elusive nature of these stories calls the person back to the understanding that this business of a life story is just that, a story that can never be completed.

Stories then, like the lives they tell about, are always open-ended, inconclusive and ambiguous, subject to multiple interpretations. Some are big; others are little. Some take on heroic, folktale proportions in the cultural lives of groups members; others are tragic; and all too few are comic. Some break fast and run to rapid conclusions. Most slowly unwind and twist back on themselves as persons seek to find meaning for themselves in the experiences they call their own. Some are told for the person by others who are called experts, be these journalists or professional biographers. Some the person keeps to himself or herself and tells no one else. Many individuals are at a loss as to what story to tell, feeling that they have nothing worthwhile to talk about. Within this group, there are persons who have no voice and no one to tell their story to.

This means that biographical work must always be interventionist, seeking to give notice to those who may otherwise not be allowed to tell their story or who are denied a voice to speak (see Bertaux, 1981, p. 6). This is what "écriture feminine" attempts; a radical form of feminist writing which "transgresses structures of domination — a kind of writing which reproduces the struggle for voice of those on the wrong side of the power relationship" (Clough, 1988, p. 3). This stance disrupts the classic oedipal logic of the life history method which situated subjectivity and self-development in the patriarchal system of marriage, kinship, and sexuality. This logic, as argued in Chapters 2 and 3, underwrites the scientistic, positivistic use of life histories and supports institutionalized sociological discourse on human subjects as individuals who can tell true stories about their lives (see Clough, 1988, p. 13). "Écriture feminine," moving from a deconstructive stance, makes no attempt at the production of biographical narratives which fill out the sociologist's version of what a life and its stories should look like. It accepts sociology as fictive writing and biographical work as the search for partial, not full, identities (Clough, 1988, p. 14).

Students of the method must begin to assemble a body of work that is grounded in the workings of these various cultural groups. This is the challenge and the promise of this project. If we are to speak to the Fourth Epoch, as Mills (1959) called the postmodern period, then we must begin to listen to the workings of these groups that make up our time. We must learn how to connect biographies and lived experiences, the epiphanies of lives, to the groups and social relationships that surround and shape persons.[1]

As we write about lives, we bring the world of others into our texts. We create differences, oppositions, and presences which allow us to maintain the illusion that we have captured the "real" experiences of "real" people. In fact, we create the persons we write about, just as they create themselves when they engage in storytelling practices. As students of the biographical method, we must become more sensitive to the writing strategies we use when we attempt to accomplish these ends. And, as readers, we can only have trust or mistrust in the writers that we read, for there is no way to stuff a real-live person between the two covers of a text.

Biographical studies should attempt to articulate how each subject deals with the problems of coherence, illusion, consubstantiality, presence, deep inner selves, others, gender, class, starting and ending points, epiphanies, fictions, truths, and final causes. These recurring, obdurate, culturally constructed dimensions of Western lives provide framing devices for the stories that are told about the lives that we study. They are, however, no more than artifices, contrivances that writers and tellers are differentially skilled at using. As writers we must not be trapped into thinking that they are any more than cultural conventions.

As we learn to do this, we must remember that our primary obligation is always to the people we study, not to our project or to a larger discipline. The lives and stories that we hear and study are given to us under a promise, that promise being that we protect those who have shared with us. And, in return, this sharing will allow us to write life documents that speak to the human dignity, the suffering, the hopes, the dreams, the lives gained, and the lives lost by the people we study. These documents will become testimonies to the ability of the human being to endure, to prevail, and to triumph over the structural forces that threaten at any moment to annihilate all of us. If we foster the illusion that we understand when we do not or that we have found meaningful, coherent lives where none exist, then we engage in a cultural practice that is just as repressive as the most repressive of political regimes.

NOTES

1. The phrase "pathography" has been recently coined to describe those culturally based, popular autobiographies that draw upon a member's condition, or pathology, like alcoholism, mental illness, child abuse, or sexual violence. With this word, like its television counterpart, "docudrama," a story is reduced to a category which has a ready-made readership in the larger marketplace of cultural consumers.

REFERENCES

Adler, Patricia A. and Peter Adler (1987) Membership Roles in Field Research. Newbury Park, CA: Sage.

Aladjem, Sonia (1987) "Structures of the Self: A Study of the Female Life Cycle Through Autobiographies of Representative French Authors." Unpublished doctoral dissertation, Loyola University of Chicago.

Alcoholics Anonymous (1976) Alcoholics Anonymous: The Story of How Many Thousands of Men and Women Have Recovered From Alcoholism, 3rd edition. New York: Alcoholics Anonymous World Services, Inc.

Allport, Gordon W. (1942) The Use of Personal Documents in Psychological Research. New York: Social Science Research Council.

Althusser, Louis (1971) Lenin and Philosophy. New York: Monthly Review Press.

Augustine, St. (1960) The Confessions. New York: Doubleday.

Balbus, Issac D. (1986) "Disciplining Women: Michel Foucault and the Power of Feminist Discourse." Praxis International 5: 465-483.

Balsamo, Anne (1988) "Reading Cyborgs Writing Feminism." Communication 10: 331-344.

Barnes, Julian (1987) Flaubert's Parrot. New York: Knopf.

Barthes, Roland (1957/1972) Mythologies. New York: Hill and Wang.

Becker, Howard S. (1966) "Introduction," pp. v-xvii in Clifford Shaw, The Jack-Roller. Chicago: University of Chicago Press.

Becker, Howard S. (1986) Doing Things Together: Selected Papers. Evanston, IL: Northwestern University Press.

Bell, Quentin (1972) Virginia Woolf: A Biography. New York: Harcourt Brace Jovanovich.

Benveniste, E. (1966) Problems in General Linguistics. Coral Gables, FL: University of Miami Press.

Bertaux, Daniel (1981a) "Introduction," pp. 1-15 in Daniel Bertaux (ed.) Biography and Society: The Life History Approach in the Social Sciences. Beverly Hills, CA: Sage.

Bertaux, Daniel, (ed.) (1981b) Biography and Society: The Life History Approach in the Social Sciences. Beverly Hills, CA: Sage.

Bertaux, Daniel (1987) "Review Essay of L'illusion biographique" by Pierre Bourdieu (Acts de la recherche en sciences sociales 62/63: 69-72) in Life Stories/Récits de vie 3: 47-50.

Bertaux, Daniel and Martin Kohli (1984) "The Life Story Approach: A Continental View." Annual Review of Sociology 10: 215-237.

Blumer, Herbert (1979) "Introduction to the Transaction Edition." Critiques of Research in the Social Sciences: An Appraisal of Thomas and Znaniecki's The Polish Peasant in Europe and America. New Brunswick, NJ: Transaction Books.

Blumer, Herbert (1969) Symbolic Interactionism. Englewood Cliffs, NJ: Prentice Hall.

Blumer, Herbert (1939) Critique of Research in the Social Sciences I: An Appraisal of Thomas and Znaniecki's *Polish Peasant*. New York: Social Science Research Council.

Bogdan, Robert (1974) Being Different: The Autobiography of Jane Fry. London: John Wiley.

Bourdieu, Pierre (1986) "L'illusion biographique." Acts de la Recherche en Sciences Sociales 62/63: 69-72.

Brown, Richard Harvey (1987) Society as Text: Essays on Rhetoric, Reason and Reality. Chicago: University of Chicago Press.

Bruner, Edward M. (1984) "The Opening up of Anthropology," pp. 1-18 in Edward M. Bruner (ed.) Text, Play, and Story: The Construction and Reconstruction of Self and Society. Washington, D.C.: The American Ethnological Society.

Bruner, Edward M. (1986) "Experience and Its Expressions," pp. 3-32 in Victor W. Turner and Edward M. Bruner (eds.) The Anthropology of Experience. Urbana, IL: University of Illinois Press.

Bruss, Elizabeth (1976) Autobiographical Acts. Baltimore: Johns Hopkins.

Bulmer, Martin (1984) The Chicago School of Sociology. Chicago: University of Chicago Press.

Burgess, Ernest (1930/1966) "Discussion," pp. 185-197 in Clifford Shaw *The Jack-Roller*. Chicago: University of Chicago Press.

Camargo, Aspasia (1985) "The Life History Approach in Latin America." Life Stories/Récits de vie 1:41-53.

Carey, James T. (1975) Sociology and Public Affairs. Beverly Hills, CA: Sage.

Carver, Raymond (1988a) "Gravey." The New Yorker 29 August: 28.

Carver, Raymond (1988b) "Obituary." The New York Times 3 August: 11.

Carver, Raymond (1988c) Where I'm Calling From: New and Selected Stories. New York: Atlantic Monthly Press.

Cheever, Susan (1984) Home Before Dark: A Biographical Memoir of John Cheever by His Daughter. Boston: Houghton Mifflin.

Clifford, James (1988) The Predicament of Culture: Twentieth-Century Ethnography, Literature, and Art. Cambridge, MA: Harvard University Press.

Clifford, James and George E. Marcus (eds.) (1986) Writing Culture: The Poetics and Politics of Ethnography. California: University of California Press.

Clough, Patrica Ticineto (1988) "Women Writing and the Life History: A Reading of Toni Morrison's "The Bluest Eye." Unpublished manuscript.

Clough, Patricia Ticineto (1989) "The Deconstruction of Ethnographic Subjectivity and the Construction of Deliberate Belief." Forthcoming in Studies in Symbolic Interaction 11.

Cockshut, A. O. J. (1984) The Art of Autobiography. New Haven, CT: Yale University Press.

Corradi, Consuelo (1987) "Hermeneutic Itineraries of *The Polish Peasant*." Unpublished doctoral dissertation, University of Rome, Italy.

Coser, Lewis A. (1986) Masters of Sociological Thought: Ideas in Historical and Social Context, 2nd edition. New York: Harcourt Brace Jovanovich.

Crapanzano, Vincent (1980) Tuhami: Portrait of a Moroccan. Chicago: University of Chicago Press.

Culler, Jonathan (1981) The Pursuit of Signs: Semiotics, Literature, Deconstruction. Ithaca, NY: Cornell University Press.

Davis, Natalie Zemon (1986) "Boundaries and the Sense of Self in Sixteenth-Century France," pp. 53-63 in Thomas C. Heller, Morton Sosna, and David E. Wellbery (eds.) Reconstructing Individualism: Autonomy, Individuality, in Western Thought. Stanford, CA: Stanford University Press.

de Lauretis, Tersa (1987) Technologies of Gender: Essays on Theory, Film and Fiction. Bloomington, IN: Indiana University Press.

Denzin, Norman K. (1989a) Interpretive Interactionism. Newbury Park, CA: Sage.

Denzin, Norman K. (1989b) The Research Act, 3rd edition. Englewood Cliffs, NJ: Prentice Hall.

Denzin, Norman K. (1989c) "Reading Tender Mercies: Two Interpretations," The Sociological Quarterly 30: 37-57.

Denzin, Norman K. (1989d) "Reading Derrida: Cultural Studies and Doing the Sociology of Knowledge." Current Perspectives in Social Theory (in press).

Denzin, Norman K. (1988) "Act, Language and Self in Symbolic Interactionist Thought," Studies in Symbolic Interaction 9: 51-80.

Denzin, Norman K. (1987a) The Alcoholic Self. Newbury park, CA: Sage.

Denzin, Norman K. (1987b) The Recovering Alcoholic. Newbury Park, CA: Sage.

Denzin, Norman K. (1987c) "Under the Influence of Time: Reading the Interactional Text," The Sociological Quarterly 28 (Fall): 327-342.

Denzin, Norman K. (1987d) "On Semiotics and Symbolic Interaction," Symbolic Interaction 10 (Spring): 1-20.

Denzin, Norman K. (1987e) "The Death of Sociology in the 1980s." American Journal of Sociology 93 (July): 175-180.

Denzin, Norman K. (1986a) "Postmodern Social Theory." Sociological Theory 4 (Winter): 194-204.

Denzin, Norman K. (1986b) "Interpretive Interactionism and the Use of Life Stories." Revista Internacional de Sociologia 44 (July-September): 321-339.

Denzin, Norman K. (1986c) "Interpreting the Lives of Ordinary People: Sartre, Heidegger, Faulkner." Life Stories/Récits de vie 2: 6-19.

Denzin, Norman K. (1986d) "Reinterpreting The Polish Peasant," pp. 61-74 in Zygmunt Dulczewski (ed.) A Commemorative Book in Honor of Florian Znaniecki on the Centenary of His Birth. Posnan, Poland: Uniwersytetus Im. Adama Mickiewicza.

Denzin, Norman K. (1985) "A Controversy over Method versus Meaning in Interpreting Life History Materials." Biographie et Société/Biography and Society Newsletter 4: 5-10.

Denzin, Norman K. (1984a) On Understanding Emotion. San Francisco: Jossey-Bass.

Denzin, Norman K. (1984b) "Interpreting the Biography and Society Life Story Project." Biographie et Société/Biography and Society Newsletter 2: 4-5.

Denzin, Norman K. (1983) "Interpretive Interactionism," pp. 129-146 in Gareth Morgan (ed.) Beyond Method: Strategies for Social Research. Beverly Hills, CA: Sage.

Denzin, Norman K. (1978) The Research Act, 2nd edition. New York: McGraw-Hill.

Denzin, Norman K. (1977) "Notes on the Criminogenic Hypothesis: A Case Study of the American Liquor Industry." American Sociological Review 42 (December): 905-920.

Denzin, Norman K. (1970) The Research Act: A Theoretical Introduction to Sociological Methods, 1st edition. Chicago: Aldine.

Derrida, Jacques (1972) "Structure, Sign and Play in the Discourse of the Human Sciences," pp. 247-265 in Richard Macksey and Eugene Donato (eds.) The Structuralist Controversy: The Languages of Criticism and the Sciences of Man. Baltimore, MD: Johns Hopkins University Press. (Reprinted in Derrida, 1967/1978).

Derrida, Jacques (1967/73) Speech and Phenomena. Evanston, IL: Northwestern University Press.

Derrida, Jacques (1967/76) Of Grammatology. Baltimore, MD: Johns Hopkins University Press.

Derrida, Jacques (1967/78) Writing and Difference. Chicago: University of Chicago Press.

Derrida, Jacques (1972/81) Positions. Chicago: University of Chicago Press.

Derrida, Jacques (1987) "Women in the Beehive: A Seminar," pp. 189-203 in Alice Jardine and Paul Smith (eds.) Men in Feminism. New York: Routledge.

Dilthey, Wilhelm (1910/63) "Autobiography and History," pp. 85-93 in Wilhelm Dilthey (1962) Pattern and Meaning in History: Thoughts on History and Sociology, edited with an Introduction by H. P. Rickman. New York: Harper & Row.

Dilthey, Wilhelm (1900/1976) Selected Writings (H. P. Rickman, editor and translator). Cambridge, UK: Cambridge University Press.

Dolby-Stahl, Sandra K. (1985) "A Folkloristic Methodology for the Study of Meaning in Personal Narrative." Journal of Folklore Research 22: 45-70.

Dollard, John (1935) Criteria for the Life History. New Haven, CT: Yale University Press.

Douglas, Jack D. (1985) Creative Interviewing. Newbury Park, CA: Sage.

Douglas, Jack D. and Freda Cruse Atwell (1988) Love, Intimacy, and Sex. Newbury Park, CA: Sage.

Douglas, Jack D. and John Johnson (eds.) (1977) Existential Sociology. New York: Cambridge.

Dulczewski, Zygmunt (ed.) (1986) A Commemorative Book in Honor of Florian Znaniecki on the Centenary of His Birth. Posnan, Poland: Uniwersytetus Im. Adama Mickiewicza.

Durkheim, Emile (1912) The Elementary Forms of the Religious Life. London: Allen and Unwin.

Elbaz, Robert (1987) The Changing Nature of the Self: A Critical Study of The Autobiographical Discourse. Iowa City: University of Iowa Press.

Ellman, Richard (1959) James Joyce. New York: Oxford University Press.

Faris, Robert E. L. (1967) Chicago Sociology: 1920-1932. San Francisco: Chandler.

Feibleman, Peter (1988) Lilly: Reminiscences of Lillian Hellman. New York: William Morrow.

Foucault, Michel (1980) Power/Knowledge: Selected Interviews and Other Writings, 1972-1977. New York: Pantheon.

Frank, Arthur W. (1985) "Out of Ethnomethodology," pp. 101-116 in H. J. Helle and S. J. Eisenstadt (eds.) Micro-Sociological Theory. Newbury Park, CA: Sage.

Freccero, John (1986) "Autobiography and Narrative," pp. 16-29 in Thomas C. Heller, Morton Sosna, and David A. Wellbery (eds.) Reconstructing Individualism: Autonomy, Individuality, in Western Thought. Stanford, CA: Stanford University Press.

Gadamer, H. G. (1976) Truth and Method. London: Sheed and Ward.

Garfinkel, Harold (1967) Studies in Ethnomethodology. Englewood Cliffs, NJ: Prentice Hall.

Garfinkel, Harold (1988) "Evidence for Locally Produced, Naturally Accountable Phenomena of Order, Logic, Reason, Meaning, Method, etc., in and as of the Essential

Quiddity of Immortal Ordinary Society, (I of IV): An Announcement of Studies."
Sociological Theory 6: 103-109.

Geertz, Clifford (1988) Works and Lives: The Anthropologist as Author. Stanford, CA:
Stanford University Press.

Geertz, Clifford (1983) Local Knowledge. New York: Basic Books.

Geiger, S. N. G. (1986) "Women's Life Histories: Method and Content." Signs 11
(Winter): 334-351.

Glaser, Barney G. and Anselm L. Strauss (1967) The Discovery of Grounded Theory.
Chicago: Aldine.

Goffman, Erving (1974) Frame Analysis. New York: Harper and Row.

Gottschalk, Louis, Clyde Kluckhohn, and Robert Angell (1945) The Use of Personal
Documents in History, Anthropology, and Sociology. New York: Social Science
Research Council.

Gusdorf, George (1980) "Conditions and Limits of Autobiography," pp. 28-48 in James
Olney (ed.) Autobiography: Essays Theoretical and Critical. Princeton, NJ: Princeton
University Press.

Hall, John R. (1987) Gone From the Promised Land: Jonestown in American Cultural
History. New Brunswick, NJ: Transaction Books.

Hall, Stuart (1980) "Cultural Studies and the Centre: Some Problematics and Problems,"
pp. 1-49 in S. Hall, D. Hobson, A. Lowe, and P. Willis (eds.) Culture, Media, and
Language: Working Papers in Cultural Studies.

Hall, Stuart (1987) "Questions and Answers," pp. 58-73 in Cary Nelson and Lawrence
Grossberg (eds.) Marxism and the Interpretation of Culture. Urbana, IL: University
of Illinois Press.

Hegel, G. W. F. (1807/1931) The Phenomenology of Mind. London: Allen and Unwin.

Heidegger, Martin (1962) Being and Time. New York: Harper and Row.

Helling, Ingeborg K. (1988) "The Life History Method: A Survey and a Discussion with
Norman K. Denzin." Studies in Symbolic Interaction 9: 211-243.

Helling, Ingeborg K. (1987) "On 'The Bias of Method over Meaning or Interpretation in
Biography and Society Investigations': A Discussion with Norman K. Denzin."
Biography and Society Newsletter 8: 71-78.

Helling, Ingeborg K. (1984) "The State of Biographical Research in German-Speaking
Sociology." Biography and Society Newsletter 3: 12-20.

Hellman, Lillian (1970) An Unfinished Woman. Boston: Little, Brown.

Hellman, Lillian (1973) Pentimento. Boston: Little, Brown.

Hellman, Lillian (1976) Scoundrel Time. Boston: Little, Brown.

Heyl, Barbara Sherman (1979) The Madame as Entrepreneur: Career Management in
House Prostitution. New Brunswick, NJ: Transaction Books.

Homans, George (1969) "A Life of Synthesis," pp. 13-34 in Irving Louis Horowitz (ed.)
Sociological Self-Images: A Collective Portrait. Beverly Hills, CA: Sage.

Homans, George (1962) Sentiments and Activities. New York: Free Press.

Horowitz, Irving Louis (1969) "Introduction," pp. 9-12 in Irving Louis Horowitz (ed.),
Sociological Self-Images: A Collective Portrait. Beverly Hills, CA: Sage.

Husserl, Edmund (1913/1962) Ideas: General Introduction to Pure Phenomenology. New
York: Collier Books.

James, William (1890/1950) The Principles of Psychology. New York: Dover.

Jameson, Fredric (1975-76) "The Ideology of the Text." Salmagundi 31/32: 204-06.

Jelinek, Estelle C. [ed.] (1980) Women's Autobiography: Essays in Criticism. Bloomington, IN: Indiana University Press.

Kanfer, Stefan (1988) "Review of Lilly: Reminiscences of Lillian Hellman" by Peter Feibleman. (New York: William Morrow) New York Times Book Review 11 September: 15-16, 18.

Kellerman, Stewart (1988) "Raymond Carver, Writer and Poet of the Working Poor, Dies at 50," The New York Times 3 August: 11.

Kohli, Martin (1987) "Report on Research Activities." Biography and Society Newsletter 8: 79-80.

Kohli, Martin (1986) "Biographical Research in the German Language Area," pp. 91-110 in Zygmunt Dulczewski (ed.) A Commemorative Book in Honor of Florian Znaniecki on the Centenary of His Birth. Posnan, Poland: Uniwersytetus Im. Adama Mickiewicza.

Kohli, Martin (1981) "Biography: Account, Text, Method," pp. 61-76 in Daniel Bertaux (ed.) Biography and Society: The Life History Approach in the Social Sciences. Beverly Hills, CA: Sage.

Kristeva, Julia (1974) La Révolution du Langage Poétique. Paris: Editions du Seuil.

Lacan, Jacques (1977) Ecrits: A Selection (A. Sheridan, translator) New York: Norton.

Lemert, Charles C. (1986) "Whole Life Social Theory: A discussion of I. L. Horowitz, C. Wright Mills: An American Utopian, and G. C. Homans, Coming to My Senses: An Autobiography of a Sociologist." Theory and Society 15: 431-442.

Lemert, Edwin, A. (1951) Social Pathology. New York: McGraw Hill.

Lesser, Wendy (1988) "Autobiography and the 'I' of the Beholder." The New York Times Book Review 27 November: 1, 26-28.

Lewis, Oscar (1970) The Children of Sanchez: Autobiography of a Mexican Family. London: Penguin Books.

Lewis, Oscar (1969) La Vida. Mexico: Moritz.

Lindesmith, Alfred, Anselm L. Strauss and Norman K. Denzin (1988) Social Psychology, 6th edition. Englewood Cliffs, NJ: Prentice Hall.

Manning, Peter K. (1987) Semiotics and Fieldwork. Newbury Park, CA: Sage.

Martindale, Don (1981) The Nature and Types of Sociological Theory, 2nd edition. Boston: Houghton Mifflin.

Marx, Karl (1852/1983) "From the Eighteenth Brumaire of Louis Bonaparte," pp. 287-323 in E. Kamenka (ed.) The Portable Karl: Marx. New York: Penguin.

McCall, Michal (1989) "The Significance of Storytelling." Studies in Symbolic Interaction 11: In press.

McCall, Michal (1985) "Life History and Social Change." Studies in Symbolic Interaction 6: 169-182.

McCall, Michal and Judith Wittner (1988) "The Good News About Life History." Presented to the 1988 Annual Symposium of The Society for the Study of Symbolic Interaction, Chicago, Illinois, 29 April.

Mehlman, Jeffrey. (1974) A Structural Study of Autobiography. Ithaca, NY: Cornell University Press.

Merleau-Ponty, Maurice (1968) The Visible and the Invisible. Evanston, IL: Northwestern University Press.

Merleau-Ponty, Maurice (1964) Signs. Evanston, IL: Northwestern University Press.

Merton, Robert K. and Matilda White Riley (eds.) (1980) Sociological Traditions From Generation to Generation. Norwood, NJ: Ablex.

Mills, C. Wright (1959) The Sociological Imagination. New York: Oxford.

Misch, Georg (1951) A History of Autobiography in Antiquity, Vol. I. Cambridge, MA: Harvard University Press.

Montaigne, Michel de (1572-1588/1958) The Complete Essays of Montaigne, translated by Donald M. Frame. Stanford, CA: Stanford University Press.

Neal, Patricia (with Richard DeNeut). (1988) As I Am: An Autobiography. New York: Simon and Schuster.

New York Times, Obituary Section, 1988. 20 July: 50.

New York Times, Book Review Section. 1988. 24 July.

Oevermann, U. et al. (1979) "Die Methodologie einer 'objektiven' Hermeneutik und ihre allgemeine forschungslogische Bedeuting in den Sozialwissenschaften," pp. 352-434 in H. G. Soeffner (ed.) Interpretative Verfahren in den Sozial—und Textwissenschaften. Stuttgart, Germany: Metzler.

Park, Robert E. (1952) "Human Communities," pp. 110-116 in Everett C. Hughes et al. (eds.) The City and Human Ecology. Glencoe, IL: Free Press.

Pascal, Roy (1960) Design and Truth in Autobiography. Cambridge, MA: Harvard University Press.

Peirce, Charles S. (1959) Collected Papers, Vol. 8. Cambridge, MA: Belknap Press of Harvard University Press.

Peirce, Charles S. (1958) Charles S. Peirce: Selected Writings. (Edited with an introduction and notes by Philip P. Wiener.) New York: Dover.

Perinbanayagam, Robert S. (1985) Signifying Acts. Carbondale, IL: Southern Illinois University Press.

Peterson, Linda H. (1986) Victorian Autobiography: The Tradition of Self-Interpretation. New Haven, CT: Yale University Press.

Plath, David W. (1987) "Making Experience Come out Right: Culture as Biography." Central Issues in Anthropology 7: 1-8.

Plath, David W. (1980) Long Engagements: Maturity in Modern Japan. Stanford, CA: Stanford University Press.

Plummer, Ken (1983) Documents of Life. London: Allen and Unwin.

Radway, Janet (1987) "Power, Control and Ideology in The Book-of-the-Month Club." Lecture given to the Unit for Criticism and Interpretive Theory, University of Illinois, Urbana, 13 April, 1987.

Radway, Janet (1984) Reading the Romance: Women, Patriarchy, and Popular Literature. Chapel Hill, NC: University of North Carolina Press.

Renza, Louis A. (1977) "The Veto of the Imagination: A Theory of Autobiography." New Literary History 9: 2-26.

Ricoeur, Paul (1974) "The Question of the Subject: The Challenge of Semiology," pp. 236-266 in Paul Ricoeur The Conflict of Interpretations: Essays in Hermeneutics. Evanston, IL: Northwestern University Press.

Riemann, Gerhard and Fritz Schutze (1987) "Some Notes on a Student Research Workshop on 'Biographical Analysis, Interaction Analysis, and Analysis of Social Worlds.'" Biography & Society Newsletter 8: 54-70.

Rollyson, Carl (1988) Lillian Hellman: Her Legacy and Her Legend. New York: St. Martin's Press.

Roos, J. P. (1987) "From Farm to Office: Family, Self-Confidence and the New Middle Class." Life Stories/Récits de vie 3: 7-20.

Roth, Philip (1988) Facts: A Novelist's Autobiography. New York: Farrar, Strauss and Giroux.

Roth, Phillip (1988) The Facts. New York: Knopf.

Sartre, Jean-Paul (1987) The Family Idiot: Gustave Flaubert, Volume 2, 1821-1857. Chicago: University of Chicago Press. (Originally published 1971).

Sartre, Jean-Paul (1981) The Family Idiot: Gustave Flaubert, Volume 1, 1821-1857. Chicago: University of Chicago Press. (Originally published 1971).

Sartre, Jean-Paul (1976) Critique of Dialectical Reason. London: NLP.

Sartre, Jean-Paul (1964) The Words. New York: Vantage Books.

Sartre, Jean-Paul (1963) Search for a method. New York: Knopf.

Sartre, Jean-Paul (1952/1963) Saint Genet: Actor and Martyr. New York: Pantheon.

Sartre, Jean-Paul (1943/1956) Being and Nothingness. New York: Philosophical Library.

Sartre, Jean-Paul (1943/1978) Being and Nothingness. New York: Simon and Schuster.

Schutz, Alfred (1932/1967) The Phenomenology of the Social World. Evanston, IL: Northwestern University Press.

Schutz, Alfred and Thomas Luckmann (1973) The Structures of the Life World. Evanston, IL: Northwestern University Press.

Schutze, Fritz (1983) "Biographieforsching und Narratives Interview." Neue Praxis 3: 283-293.

Shaw, Clifford (1930/1966) The Jack-Roller. Chicago: University of Chicago Press.

Shapiro, Stephen A. (1968) "The Dark Continent of Literature: Autobiography," Comparative Literature Studies 5: 410-425.

Short, James F., Jr. (1969) "A Natural History of One Sociological Career," pp. 117-132 in Irving Louis Horowitz (ed.) Sociological Self-Images: A Collective Portrait. Beverly Hills, CA: Sage.

Simmel, Georg (1910/1950) "The Problem of Sociology." American Journal of Sociology 15: 296-97. (Reprinted in Kurt H. Wolff (ed.) (1950) The Sociology of Georg Simmel. Glencoe, IL: The Free Press.

Sloan, Ted (1987) Deciding: Self-Deception in Life-Choices. London: Methuen.

Snodgrass, Jon (1982) The Jack-Roller at Seventy: A Fifty-Year Follow-Up. Lexington, MA: Lexington Books.

Spacks, Patricia (1976) Imagining a Self: Autobiography and Novel in Eighteenth-Century England. Cambridge, MA: Harvard University Press.

Spengemann, William C. (1980) The Forms of Autobiography. New Haven, CT: Yale University Press.

Spivak, G. (1983) "Displacement and the Discourse of Woman," pp. 254-276 in Mark Krupnick (ed.) Displacement, Derrida and After. Bloomington, IN: Indiana University Press.

Springer, M. (1980) Autobiography: Essays Theoretical and Critical. Princeton, NJ: Princeton University Press.

Stahl, Sandra K. D. (1977) "The Personal Narrative as Folklore." Journal of the Folklore Institute 14: 9-30.

Stanton, D. (1984) The Female Autograph. Chicago: University of Chicago Press.

Steedman, Carolyn Kay (1987) Landscape for a Good Woman: A Story of Two Lives. New Brunswick, NJ: Rutgers University Press.

Stein, Gertrude (1960) The Autobiography of Alice B. Toklas. New York: Vintage Books.

Strauss, Anselm L. (1987) Qualitative Analysis for Social Scientists. New York: Cambridge.

Sullivan, Harry Stack (1953) The Interpersonal Theory of Psychiatry. New York: Norton.

Thomas, W. I., and Dorothy Swaine Thomas (1928) The Child in America. New York: Knopf.

Thomas, W. I. and Florian Znaniecki (1918-1920) The Polish Peasant in Europe and America. Volumes I-II. Chicago: University of Chicago Press. Volumes III-V, Boston: Badger Press.

Thompson, Paul (1978) The Voice of the Past: Oral History. Oxford, UK: Oxford University Press.

Titon, Jeff Todd (1980) "The Life Story." Journal of American Folklore 93: 276-92.

Turner, Victor W. and Edward M. Bruner (eds.) (1986) The Anthropology of Experience. Urbana, IL: University of Illinois Press.

Turner, Victor W. (1986) "Dewey, Dilthey, and Drama: An Essay in the Anthropology of Experience," pp. 33-44 in Victor W. Turner and Edward M. Bruner (eds.) The Anthropology of Experience. Urbana, IL: University of Illinois Press.

Van Maanen, John (1988) Tales of the Field. Chicago: University of Chicago Press.

Wagner, Helmut R. (1983) Alfred Schutz: An Intellectual Biography. Chicago: University of Chicago Press.

Walsh, Martin J. (1988) "Obituary." New York Times 30 July: 50.

Weber, Max (1922/1957) The Theory of Social and Economic Organization. (Translated by A. M. Henderson and Talcott Parsons.) Glencoe, IL: Free Press.

Weber, Max (1922/1947) The Methodology of the Social Sciences. (Translated by Edward M. Shils and Henry A. Finch.) Glencoe, IL: Free Press.

Wiley, Norbert (1986) "Early American Sociology and The Polish Peasant." Sociological Theory 4: 20-40.

Woolf, Virginia (1929) A Room of One's Own. London: Hogarth.

Wright, William (1986) Lillian Hellman: The Image, the Woman. New York: Simon and Schuster.

Young, Kimball (1952) Personality and Problems of Adjustment. New York: Appleton-Century-Crofts.

Zaretsky, Eli (ed.) (1984) The Polish Peasant in Europe and America by William I. Thomas and Florian Znaniecki. Urbana, IL: University of Illinois Press.

ABOUT THE AUTHOR

NORMAN K. DENZIN is currently Professor of Sociology, Communications and Humanities at the University of Illinois, Urbana-Champaign. He is the author of several books, including *Sociological Methods* (1978), *Children and Their Caretakers* (1973), *The Values of Social Science* (1973), *The Mental Patient* [with S. P. Spitzer] (1968), *Childhood Socialization* (1977), *Social Psychology*, 6th edition [with A. Lindesmith and A. Strauss] (1988), *The Research Act*, 3rd edition (1989), *On Understanding Emotion* (1984), *The Alcoholic Self* (1987), *The Recovering Alcoholic* (1987), and *Interpretive Interactionism* (1989). *The Alcoholic Self* and *The Recovering Alcoholic* were nominated for the C. Wright Mills Award in 1988. *The Alcoholic Self* won the Cooley Award from the Society for the Study of Symbolic Interaction in 1988 and was nominated for the Sorokin Award, also known as the award for Distinguished Scholarly Publication, by the American Sociological Association in 1989. Denzin is the author of over 70 articles in various academic journals. He has been the editor of *Studies in Symbolic Interaction: A Research Journal* since 1978. He is presently President of the Midwest Sociological Society and has served as Vice President of the Society for the Study of Symbolic Interaction (1976-1977) and secretary of the Social Psychology Section of the American Sociological Association (1978-1980).

Qualitative Research Methods

Series Editor
JOHN VAN MAANEN
Massachusetts Institute of Technology

Associate Editors:
Peter K. Manning, *Michigan State University*
& Marc L. Miller, *University of Washington*

1. **RELIABILITY AND VALIDITY IN QUALITATIVE RESEARCH**
   Kirk / Miller

2. **SPEAKING OF ETHNOGRAPHY**
   Agar

3. **THE POLITICS AND ETHICS OF FIELDWORK** Punch

4. **LINKING DATA**
   Fielding / Fielding

5. **THE CLINICAL PERSPECTIVE IN FIELDWORK** Schein

6. **MEMBERSHIP ROLES IN FIELD RESEARCH** Adler / Adler

7. **SEMIOTICS AND FIELDWORK**
   Manning

8. **ANALYZING FIELD REALITY**
   Gubrium

9. **GENDER ISSUES IN FIELD RESEARCH** Warren

10. **SYSTEMATIC DATA COLLECTION**
    Weller / Romney

11. **META-ETHNOGRAPHY: Synthesizing Qualitative Studies**
    Noblit / Hare

12. **ETHNOSTATISTICS: Qualitative Foundations for Quantitative Research** Gephart

13. **THE LONG INTERVIEW**
    McCracken

14. **MICROCOMPUTER APPLICATIONS IN QUALITATIVE RESEARCH**
    Pfaffenberger

15. **KNOWING CHILDREN: Participant Observation with Minors**
    Fine / Sandstrom

16. **FOCUS GROUPS AS QUALITATIVE RESEARCH (Second Edition)** Morgan

17. **INTERPRETIVE BIOGRAPHY**
    Denzin

18. **PSYCHOANALYTIC ASPECTS OF FIELDWORK**
    Hunt

19. **ETHNOGRAPHIC DECISION TREE MODELING** Gladwin

20. **WRITING UP QUALITATIVE RESEARCH** Wolcott

21. **WRITING STRATEGIES: Reaching Diverse Audiences** Richardson

22. **SELECTING ETHNOGRAPHIC INFORMANTS** Johnson

23. **LIVING THE ETHNOGRAPHIC LIFE** Rose

24. **ANALYZING VISUAL DATA**
    Ball / Smith

25. **UNDERSTANDING ETHNOGRAPHIC TEXTS**
    Atkinson

26. **DOING CRITICAL ETHNOGRAPHY**
    Thomas

Other volumes in this series listed on outside back cover